HOW *to* USE

Microsoft®
Excel 2000

Dan Gookin
Sandy Gookin

A Division of Macmillan Computer Publishing, USA
201 W. 103rd Street
Indianapolis, Indiana 46290

SAMS

Visually in **Full Color**

How to Use
Microsoft® Excel 2000

International Standard Book Number: 0-672-315386

Library of Congress Catalog Card Number: 98-88497

Printed in the United States of America

First Printing: May 1999

01   00   99   4   3   2   1

Trademarks

Warning and Disclaimer

Executive Editor
Angela Wethington

Acquisitions Editor
Stephanie J. McComb

Development Editor
Kate Shoup Welsh

Managing Editor
Lisa Wilson

Project Editor
Rebecca Mounts

Copy Editor
Tonya Maddox

Indexer
Mary Gammons

Proofreader
Mary Ellen Stephenson

Technical Editor
Kyle Bryant

Interior Design
Nathan Clement

Cover Design
Aren Howell
Nathan Clement

Layout Technicians
Lisa England
Trina Wurst

Contents at a Glance

Contents

How To Use This Book

The Complete Visual Reference

Each chapter of this book is made up of a series of short, instructional tasks, designed to help you understand all the information that you need to get the most out of your computer hardware and software.

Each task includes a series of easy-to-understand steps designed to guide you through the procedure.

 Click: Click the left mouse button once.

 Double-click: Click the left mouse button twice in rapid succession.

 Right-click: Click the right mouse button once.

 Pointer Arrow: Highlights an item on the screen you need to point to or focus on in the step or task.

 Selection: Highlights the area onscreen discussed in the step or task.

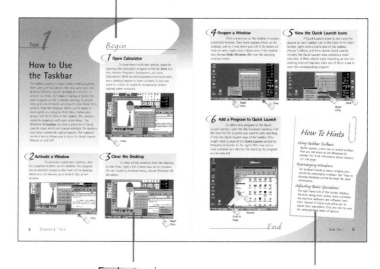

Each step is fully illustrated to show you how it looks onscreen.

Extra hints that tell you how to accomplish a goal are provided in most tasks.

 Click and Type: Click once where indicated and begin typing to enter your text or data.

Menus and items you click are shown in **bold**. Words in *italic* are defined in more detail in the glossary. Information you type is in a **special font**.

Click & Drag

Release

How to Drag: Point to the starting place or object. Hold down the mouse button (right or left per instructions), move the mouse to the new location, and then release the button.

Continues

If you see this symbol, it means the task you're in continues on the next page.

 Key icons: Clearly indicate which key combinations to use.

About the Author

Dan Gookin is the author of more than 50 books on computers, including several international bestsellers. He's the author of the original *DOS for Dummies* (IDG Books Worldwide), which sold over 4 million copies in 28 countries and began the ubiquitous *Dummies* book rage. His most recent title with Macmillan Publishing is *Dan Gookin Teaches Windows 98*. This is the first full-color book Dan's done since the fifth grade.

Sandy Gookin has been writing books for four years, although she spends most of her time raising her four boys (five if you include her husband Dan). Her first book, *Parenting For Dummies*, was given the "Seal of Quality" by The Family Channel. In between her book projects, Sandy also works as an editor. She's worked on books such as *Dan Gookin's Web Wambooli* and *C Programming for Dummies, Volume II*.

Dan and Sandy have collaborated on two other computer books, *The Illustrated Computer Dictionary for Dummies*, 3rd Edition, and *Discover Windows 95*, both from IDG Books Worldwide.

Acknowledgements

We'd like to thank fellow author Julia Kelly, who helped us confirm some notions and fears about Excel and Microsoft Access. Thanks also go to Matt Wagner, Supreme Agent of all Agents, Molly Kyle for forcing us to keep theatre in our lives, and Sandy's parents, Shirley and Virgil Hardin. We couldn't have accomplished this book as quickly as we were able to, had they not kept our boys busy playing and pumping them full of sugar.

Tell Us What You Think!

As the reader of this book, *you* are our most important critic and commentator. We value your opinion and want to know what we're doing right, what we could do better, what areas you'd like to see us publish in, and any other words of wisdom you're willing to pass our way.

As an Associate Publisher for Sams, I welcome your comments. You can fax, email, or write me directly to let me know what you did or didn't like about this book—as well as what we can do to make our books stronger.

Please note that I cannot help you with technical problems related to the topic of this book, and that due to the high volume of mail I receive, I might not be able to reply to every message.

When you write, please be sure to include this book's title and authors as well as your name and phone or fax number. I will carefully review your comments and share them with the authors and editors who worked on the book.

Fax: 317.581.4770

Email: `office_sams@mcp.com`

Mail: Angela Wethington
             Executive Editor
             Sams Publishing
             201 West 103rd Street
             Indianapolis, IN 46290 USA

Introduction

*O*ftentimes, the visual approach is the best way to learn things. We could explain and explain, but showing a picture with the how-tos right there before you solves a multitude of problems that paragraphs of text cannot. Sometimes to see it means to get it. If you're the type who appreciates that visual approach, you've found your book.

How To Use Microsoft Excel 2000, a completely colorful and visual book, entertains as it informs you about the many interesting, useful, and surprising things you can do with Microsoft's latest spreadsheet program. Our point, beyond teaching the basics of Excel, is to show you that spreadsheets mean more than numbers.

Inside this book you'll learn the following tidbits about Excel:

- ✓ How to use Excel to create fun and interesting things
- ✓ How to work with text, values, and formulas
- ✓ How to painlessly use Excel to do your math
- ✓ How to format worksheets in fun and different styles
- ✓ How to use charts
- ✓ How to spice up the worksheet with graphics
- ✓ How to use lists and the mysterious PivotTable
- ✓ How to design and read Web pages using Excel

Each topic is presented in a step-by-step method, along with plenty of images to support the text. The illustrations help you learn by showing you exactly what you're supposed to see on your screen and telling you what's important and what to ignore. Following along is fun—and entertaining.

Feel free to start anywhere in this book. Each task is self-contained, and other parts of the book are cross-referenced where necessary. Learn anything you need to know first, though you can read the book front to back if you're just starting out. Or just leave it on the coffee table to impress your friends.

They say a picture is worth a thousand words and maybe that explains why some books on Excel are so darn thick. Because this book has pictures—and lots of them—you might find it the friendliest and easiest way to move on to mastering Excel 2000 and getting the most from your computer. Welcome to *How To Use Microsoft Excel 2000*.

Task

1

Say Hello to Excel

*C*runch. Crunch. Crunch.

Supposedly, "crunch" is the sound a computer makes when it works with numbers. Words aren't as lucky. There is no word processing sound. (Clackity-clack-clack, maybe?) Nevertheless, numbers are *crunched*, and the software that does the crunching is called a *spreadsheet*. Although spreadsheets are popular, most people shun them because of the math. The mere thought of working with numbers makes some of us blanch. Here are a couple of points to make you feel better about spreadsheets:

✓ First, when you work with numbers, it's the computer that does the calculating. All you have to do is press the Enter key; the computer figures everything out for you. If you make an error, Excel is smart enough to tell you about it, even pinpointing where the error could be. That's nice.

✓ Second, Excel isn't only about numbers. A spreadsheet is really about rows and columns. Anytime you work with information that can be organized into rows or columns, you have a spreadsheet project. True, the main focus is numbers, but as you explore Excel, you'll soon discover how surprisingly right-brained it can be. Who would imagine you could design a quilt or make a calendar by using Excel? Yet those projects are merely rows and columns, which is what a spreadsheet does best. ●

How to Start Excel

There are probably half a dozen ways to start Excel. Some are obvious, while others require a little work. These steps describe the most common way to start Excel, but be sure to tune into the How-To Hints box (later in this task) for some handy alternatives.

Begin

1 Click the Start Button

The Start button is located in the lower-left corner of your desktop. Clicking the **Start** button brings up the Start menu.

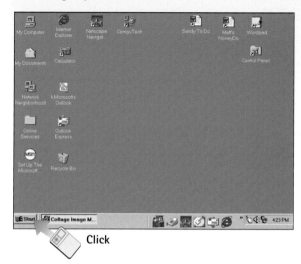

Click

2 Click Programs

Click **Programs** to view the Programs submenu. (Actually, you don't even have to click; merely hovering your mouse on the word **Programs** displays the Programs submenu.)

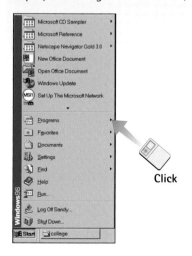

Click

3 Choose Microsoft Excel

Excel's position on the menu varies, so it may not be where it's shown in the accompanying figure. If you always look for the green **XL** icon, you should be able to find it quickly.

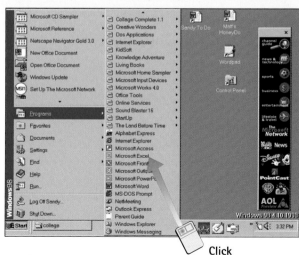

Click

4 Run the Registration Wizard

If this is the first time you've run Excel, you are asked to run the annoying Registration Wizard. You're options are to register now or register later. Do it now. (See the How-To Hints for more information about this wizard.)

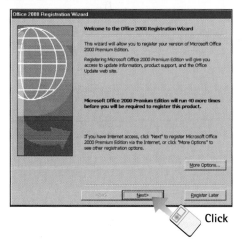

Click

5 Voilà, It's Microsoft Excel

Now your only requirement is to continue reading this book to find out what you're supposed to do with this screen full of numbers, letters, and boxes.

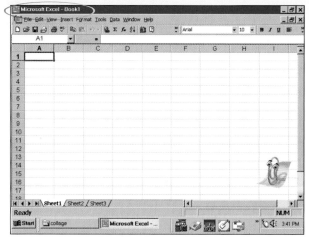

End

How-To Hints

Getting to the Start Button

If your keyboard sports a Windows key (between the Ctrl and Alt keys), you can press this key to display the Start menu.

Starting Stuff You Last Worked On

To restart a project you've been working on, look for the worksheet document's name in the Start menu's Documents submenu. Choosing the document from that menu not only starts Excel, but also loads the document, ready for action.

Registering Excel (The Annoying Wizard)

You can register Excel through the Internet, via email, or by telephone, fax, or postal mail. Follow the onscreen instructions when you first start Excel; the Registration Wizard will walk you through the steps for each method.

Putting Excel on Your Desktop

If you grow fond of Excel, you may want to put a shortcut icon on your desktop. To do this, double-click the **My Computer** icon on the desktop; then open drive C, the **Program Files** folder, and the **Microsoft Office** folder. Finally, open the **Office** folder and drag the **Excel** icon onto the desktop to create a shortcut (it's best if you minimize your window first). Don't forget to close all those windows you opened.

Putting Excel on the Quick Launch Bar

If you're using Windows 98 and have the quick launch bar visible, you can put Excel there. Just follow the steps in the previous tip, though this time drag the Excel icon to the quick launch bar instead of the desktop. (See *Dan Gookin Teaches Windows 98*, published by Que, for more information on the quick launch bar.)

How a Spreadsheet Works

A spreadsheet is a program that works with information stored in rows and columns (and no, the information need not always be numbers). It's important to know which part of the spreadsheet is what, just as when the panicked driving instructor says to "Slam on the brake!", you should know which pedal to push. The steps in this task serve more as an orientation to Excel than as steps that accomplish something in particular.

Begin

1 Excel Shows You Information

There's a lot of information on the screen. Be sure you recognize the basic parts of the program. Important elements of Excel's window are shown here; locate them on your monitor as well.

The rows and columns are important things to find on the worksheet. The rows are numbered down the left side of the screen, and columns are listed using letters along the top.

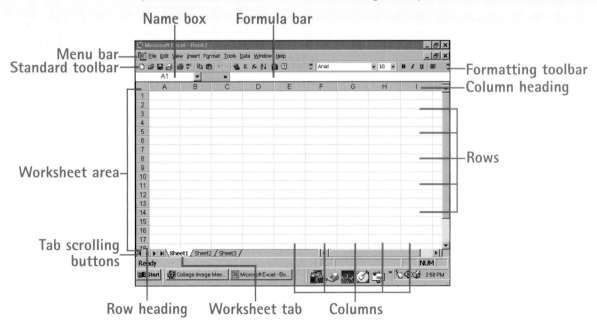

Name box   Formula bar

Menu bar
Standard toolbar

Formatting toolbar
Column heading

Worksheet area

Rows

Tab scrolling
buttons

Row heading   Worksheet tab   Columns

2 Cells

Each cubbyhole in a worksheet's grid is a *cell*. Each cell's name is derived from the row and column in which it is located. In the Excel window shown here, cell C4—which is located in row 4 of column C—is highlighted. Note that rows are numbers and columns are letters. The cell's row number and column letter appear in boldface, and the Name box contains the cell's *name*, or location.

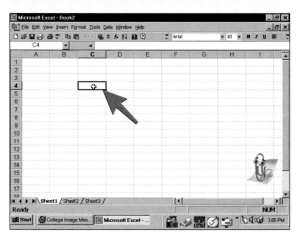

3 Cells Contain Information

A cell is a holding place for information. Cells can contain text, numbers, and even graphical patterns. They can also contain *formulas*, which display results based on the values in other cells. In this case, the information you see in the selected cell contains the total of the values above it.

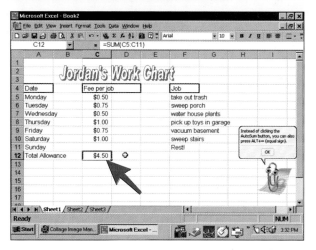

4 Change Information On-the-Fly

The beauty of the spreadsheet is that the information there can change in a second—and you can see the results instantly. This is known as a *what if*. For example, ask yourself, "What if I change my income from $32,000 a year to $320,000?" The worksheet displays the new values, telling you that someone who makes 10 times your income pays about 60 gazillion times as much in taxes.

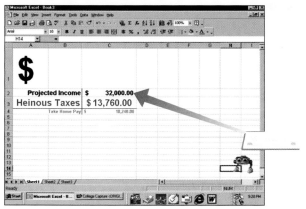

End

How-To Hints

The Third Dimension

A worksheet appears two dimensional at first, having just rows and columns, but Excel's worksheets have a third dimension as well: depth. The tabs along the bottom of the worksheet, labeled Sheet 1, Sheet 2, and Sheet 3, represent different pages in the same worksheet. Clicking one of the sheet tabs displays that page in the worksheet.

The Name Game

Rows in a worksheet are numbered from 1 on up to...well, almost infinity. The columns are lettered from A through Z, then AA through ZZ, then...who knows! Although most of the time your worksheets will be small, worksheets can get very, very big. This is no problem, provided your PC has lots of memory.

How to Use the Office Assistant

Say hello to your new friend, the Excel Office Assistant. He's the one to ask when you're scratching your head, wondering what to do next. He is the "Help" in Excel 2000. The only problem with this little guy is that you have to be pretty specific about your question. To ask, "How do I get that thing to go over to the other thing?" just isn't going to hack it.

Begin

1 Summon the Office Assistant

The Office Assistant is normally visible in Excel, but you can summon it if it's not. To summon the Office Assistant, click the **Help** button on the standard toolbar and then click **Show the Office Assistant**.

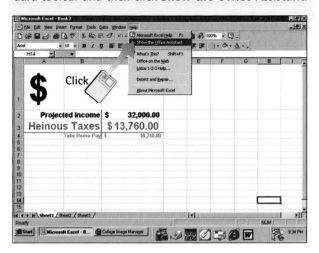

2 Using the Office Assistant

To use the Office Assistant, click your little guy (paperclip or whatever character may be on your screen). A pop-up bubble appears; merely type your question and click the **Search** button.

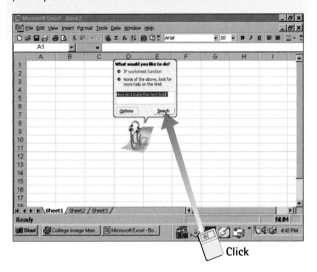

3 Click the Search Button

You can either press the **Search** button or press **Enter** after you type your question. The Office Assistant searches for the answer to your question. A list pops up to better define your question.

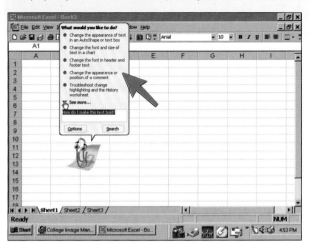

4 Choose the Best Match

Either click the topic that seems the most promising or type a new question in the box.

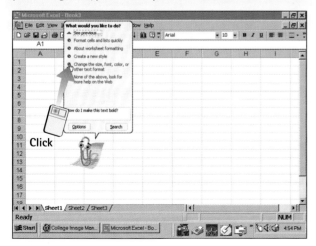

Click

5 Read the Help

You'll eventually see a Help window displayed, explaining how to accomplish a task or listing even more information. Click the colored text to see a term defined; click underlined text to view more detailed information on that topic.

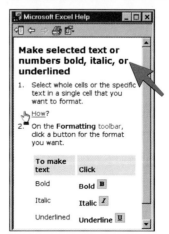

6 Close the Help Window

Click the × button in the Help window's upper-right corner to close it. You can then continue to use Excel full-screen.

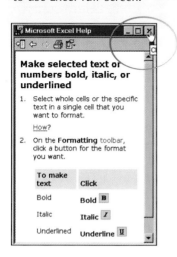

End

How-To Hints

Taking a Suggestion

The Office Assistant is observant. At times, it may notice what you're doing and offer a suggestion. When it does, you'll see a light bulb appear over its head. Click the light bulb for smidgens of information or advice.

Getting Rid of the Office Assistant

To banish the Office Assistant, right-click it and choose **Hide** from the pop-up menu. Bye!

Changing the Office Assistant

To see the complete rogue's gallery of Office Assistants, right-click your Office Assistant and select **Choose Assistant**. Click the **Next** or **Back** buttons until you find a suitable assistant and then click **OK**.

TASK **4**

How to Start a New Workbook

When you start Excel, you'll automatically be given a clean, new worksheet (page one of a workbook). That's nice, but there may be times when you are inspired and need to start a worksheet in a new workbook.

Begin

1 Workbooks Versus Worksheet

A workbook is almost the same thing as a worksheet. The reason it's called a *workbook* is because there are several pages of worksheets in each workbook. So while you're working on a worksheet, it and all its fellow worksheet pages are collectively called a workbook. Oh, semantics...

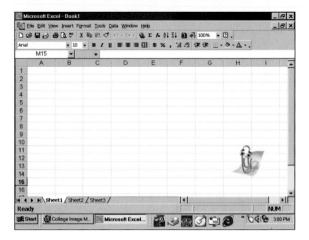

2 Choose New from the File Menu

In Excel, open the **File** menu and choose **New**.

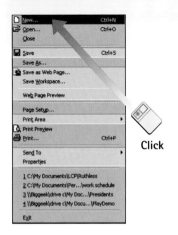

3 Choose a Workbook Template

Unless you've created additional templates, there should be only one icon found in the General tab: Workbook. Click the **Workbook** icon to select it. Once you've selected a template, the preview panel will give you an idea of what the spreadsheet might look like.

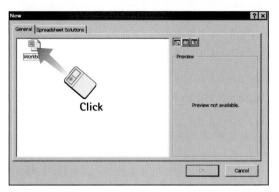

10 CHAPTER 1: SAY HELLO TO EXCEL

4 Click OK

The new workbook appears as a new window on the screen. You can see that you have a new workbook by the description at the top of the window. It will say **Book**, followed by a number. Note that unlike older versions of Excel, each new workbook is given its own program window—not a "window within a window."

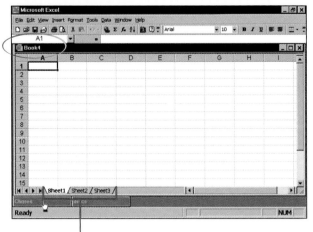

These individual
worksheets together
make a workbook

End

How-To Hints

Shortcuts

A quick way to create a new window without bothering with the New dialog box is to click the **New** button on the standard toolbar. Zap! Instant window. Alternatively, you can simply press **Ctrl+N** on the keyboard.

Switching Workbooks

Since Excel's workbooks act like separate programs in Windows, you can switch between them just as you would switch between any two Windows programs: Use the **Alt+Tab** key combination or click the workbook's button on the taskbar.

Spreadsheet Solutions

The Spreadsheet Solutions tab contains Microsoft-supplied templates that help you create specific types of worksheets.

How to Open a Workbook

Not everything you do in Excel is done from scratch. In fact, most of the work you do will be on worksheets you've already created. Those worksheets have been saved to disk, stored there like a permanent record. If you like, you can open those worksheet documents, putting them back into Excel to be changed, printed, or merely gawked at. This is all done through the Open command, a standard feature in all Windows programs.

Begin

1 Choose Open from the File Menu

In Excel, open the **File** menu (found in the taskbar at the top of your screen) and choose **Open**.

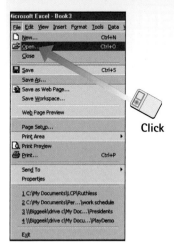

Click

2 Hunt for Your Document

The Open dialog box appears. Your job is to find the workbook document you want to open. At least some of your workbooks can probably be found in the My Documents folder. You can always choose other disk drives to look in from the Look In drop-down list.

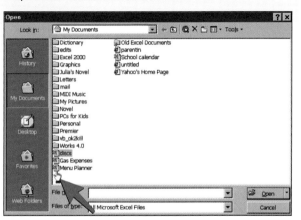

3 Select Your Workbook

When you find the workbook you want to open, click it and then click the **Open** button. You can also double-click the folder and look for workbooks. Now get to work!

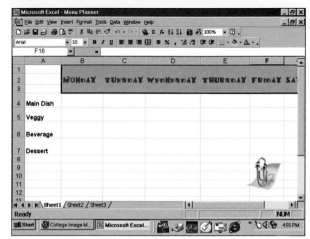

4 Find Excel Files

Excel files are the ones with the Excel icon by the filename. If the file has any other icon next to it, it's not an Excel file. To be sure that you see only Excel files in the Open dialog box, choose **Microsoft Excel Files** from the **Files of Type** drop-down list.

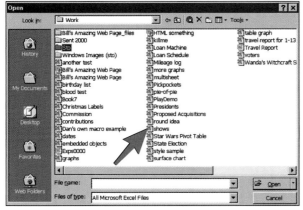

End

How-To Hints

Using Ctrl+O

You can quickly summon the Open dialog box with the handy **Ctrl+O** keyboard shortcut. This is the same as selecting **Open** from the **File** menu.

The Open Button

Another quick tool is the Open button on the toolbar. Clicking this button takes you directly to the Open dialog box.

Double-Click to Open Quick

You don't have to select a file and then click the Open button in the Open dialog box in order to open that file. Instead, you can also just double-click the file in the Open dialog box.

Opening a Web Document

Excel 2000 can also open a Web page document as a spreadsheet. Weird, huh? To do so, choose **All Microsoft Excel Files** from the **Files of Type** drop-down list in the Open dialog box. Any Web page icons you see in the file list can then be opened by Excel for whatever devious purposes thrill you.

How to Enter Data into a Cell

Information in the worksheet is stored in cells. Like the vast wall of mailboxes in the post office, every cell has an address and the potential to hold something. You pick the cell's location and then put something into it (though unlike a P.O. box, a cell in Excel can hold more than just mail).

Begin

1 Select a Cell

Click the mouse on a cell to select it; just point and click. Unlike a word processor, you can click and type anywhere on a worksheet. The selected cell is highlighted with a border so you can find it quickly. Starting a worksheet with cell B2 is a good idea, since it gives you a row and column on the top and left side of the cell to add titles or headings.

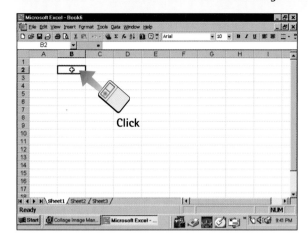

2 Type Information in the Cell

Use your keyboard to enter information in the cell. You can type in text, a numeric value, or a formula (*equation*). You'll find more information on what to type in Chapter 2, "Working the Worksheet."

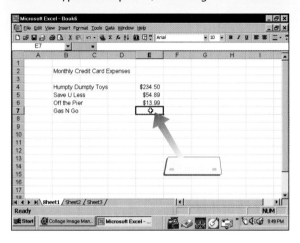

3 Move Down One Cell

When you're done typing data, press the **Enter** key to move down one cell.

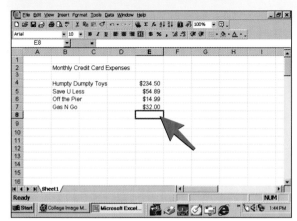

4 Move Over One Cell

When you're done typing data, press the **Tab** key to move one cell to the right. Numbers typed into a cell are automatically right-justified.

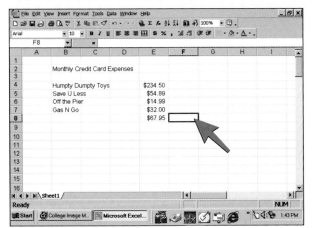

End

How-To Hints

Getting the Right Position

Trying to pluck out the "perfect" cell to start your worksheet need not be a bother. You can always insert rows or columns of new cells into the worksheet later. Chapter 2 shows you how.

Don't Worry About Formatting Yet

Excel has powerful commands that format a cell's contents. Chapter 5, "Making Your Data Presentable," and Chapter 6, "Sprucing Up the Worksheet," show you how to format your data and make your worksheet presentable.

Making the Enter Key Work "Properly"

To ensure that pressing the Enter key moves you to the next cell, open the **Tools** menu, choose **Options**, click the **Edit** tab, and put a check mark next to **Move Selection After Enter**. You have the option of where you want the cell to immediately be selected: Down, Right, Up, or Left. Click **OK**.

How to Save a Worksheet

You should always save whatever you create in a computer, even if it's silly stuff you think is unimportant. That way, a permanent copy is kept on your computer's hard drive, safe from power outages or goofs you might make. And save early; don't wait until you're "done" with a worksheet before you save. It's a good idea to save almost immediately after filling in the first cell. You should also get into the habit of resaving your stuff to disk every so often after that.

Begin

1 Choose Save As from the File Menu

If this is the first time you're saving a particular worksheet, open the **File** menu and choose **Save As**.

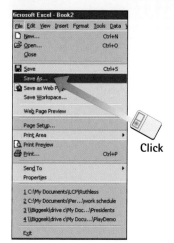

Click

2 Select a Folder for the Worksheet

The Save As dialog box appears, a standard feature of all Windows programs. You can choose where you want to save your file. Either choose another disk drive from the **Save In** drop-down list or open folders visible in the dialog box to save your workbook in that specific folder.

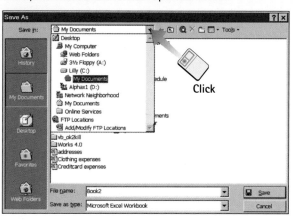

Click

3 Type the File Name

Type a short (but descriptive) name in the **File Name** text box. This is the name by which you'll recognize the file should you use the Open command later to reopen it. Clicking the **Save** button or pressing the **Enter** key saves the file.

4 Try a Different Name

Windows is fairly liberal with its file-names, allowing you to name a workbook just about anything. However, the filename must not contain the following characters: " * / : ; ? \ | < >. (Filenames can contain periods.) If you enter a filename with any of these characters, you'll see the dialog box shown here; click **OK** and try another name.

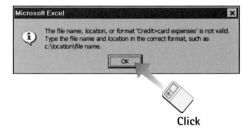

Click

5 Resave a Workbook

The first time you save a workbook, you give it a name. After that, open the **File** menu and choose **Save** to resave any changes. You can also click the **Save** button on the toolbar or use the **Ctrl+S** keyboard shortcut.

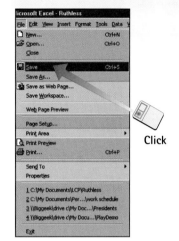

Click

End

How-To Hints

Saving Is Not Closing!

Saving a workbook is not the same thing as closing it. You can continue to work on the worksheet after you save.

Making a New Folder

You should make very descriptive folders to put your very descriptive files in. Of course, we both have a "stuff" folder for the odds and ends, but you can name folders by projects or content. To make a new folder, click the **Create New Folder** button at the top of the **Save As** dialog box. The New Folder dialog box appears. Type in the folder name under **Name**. Click **OK**.

Using Descriptive Names

Never assume that you'll remember what files with names such as **Report 7** contain. You won't. The names of folders and files should be as descriptive as you can make them. Microsoft is pretty lenient and gives you plenty of room to be creative.

How to Print a Worksheet

Printing is the ultimate joy when using a computer. It gives others solid proof that you have been working and not playing games for the past two hours. Besides, it's easier to show folks the printed hard copy of your hard work than it is to lug your computer around all over town. Printing in Excel can be very involved. This task covers printing basics only. If you want to find out all the gooey details and printing options, see Chapter 8, "Preparing the Document."

Begin

1 Preview Your Worksheet

If you want to see how the worksheet you're working on will look on paper before you actually print it, open the **File** menu and select **Print Preview**.

Click

2 Print the Previewed Worksheet

You can print the document directly from the Print Preview window; simply click the **Print** button.

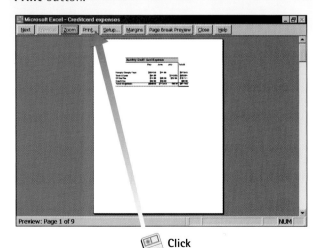

Click

3 Print from the Worksheet

If you want to print your worksheet without previewing it, begin by selecting **Print** from the **File** menu.

Click

4 Choose Print Options

The Print dialog box, which is discussed in more detail in Chapter 8, appears. For now, select the number of copies you want to print (the default is 1), click **OK**, and sit back and watch your printer spit out your document.

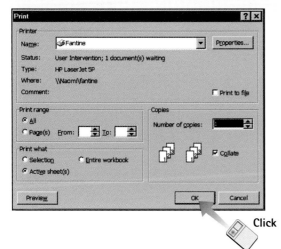

Click

End

How-To Hints

Print Quickly with the Print Tool

The quickest way to print your worksheet is to click the **Print** button on the standard toolbar. That prints your entire worksheet right away without displaying the Print dialog box.

Using the Print Command Shortcut

This is an easy one: **Ctrl+P** summons the Print dialog box just as easily as choosing **Print** from the **File** menu. Press the **Enter** key and your worksheet prints, zip-zip-zip.

Stock Your Printer

Before you print, make sure your printer is on and has plenty of paper!

How to Close a Worksheet

You'll want to close a worksheet when you are finished with it. This is not the same thing as quitting Excel outright. No—when you close a worksheet, you're putting it away without quitting Excel. You can then open something else or use the New command to start up a fresh worksheet.

Begin

1 Choose Close from the File Menu

Thwoop! Your workbook is closed, vanished from the screen—but you're still in Excel. You now have the option of starting a new worksheet (see Task 4), opening a workbook previously saved to disk (see Task 7), or quitting Excel all together (see Task 10).

Click

2 Optionally Save your File

If your workbook has yet to be saved to disk, the Office Assistant will let you know (or you'll see a warning dialog box if the Office Assistant is in hiding). Please do save your files by choosing **Yes** (refer to Task 7).

Click

3 Hide the Worksheet

If you're ready to work on something else but don't want to close this worksheet, you can minimize it. Click the **Minimize** button in the top-right corner of the window.

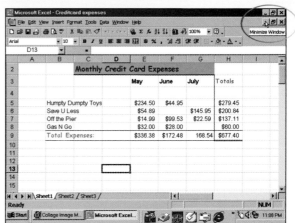

4 Reopen the Worksheet

Your worksheet disappears but is represented by a button on the taskbar. When you want to open that worksheet back up, click the button—and there she is!

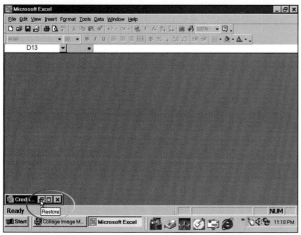

End

How-To Hints

Closing Several Open Workbooks

To close all open workbooks without quitting Excel, hold down the **Shift** key and choose **Close All** from the **File** menu.

Save Before You Close

Always save your work. You don't want to lose all that hard work you just did, so click the **save** icon on your toolbar. See Task 7 for more information on saving.

How to Quit Excel

When you're done with Excel—either for the day or for that project—quit. Of course, you don't have to quit. We leave our PCs on all the time, so if we're working on a worksheet, we just save at the end of the day. Normal people probably quit Excel more than we do. If we did ever quit, we'd most likely follow these steps.

Begin

1 Choose Exit from the File Menu

Excel closes, bringing you to the Windows desktop. If any of your workbooks haven't been saved to disk, you are asked to save them. Please do so.

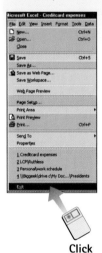

Click

2 Click the × Button

Click the × in the upper-right corner of the screen. This button is your second option for closing Excel.

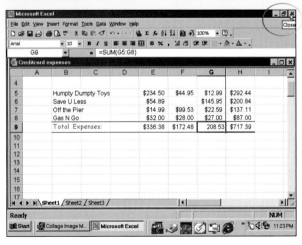

3 Save Your Work

If any of your workbooks haven't been saved to disk, you are asked to save them. Please do so.

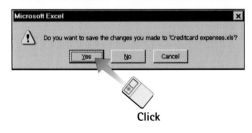

Click

4 Excel Closes

Excel closes, bringing you to the Windows desktop.

End

How-To Hints

Other Ways to Quit Excel

If choosing **Exit** from the **File** menu seems like too much mouse work, then you can press **Alt+F4**, which is a bizarre keyboard combination but works nonetheless.

Don't Quit with the Off Switch

Never quit Excel by turning off your computer. That's just not the way things are done. Turning off your PC like that is bad because it doesn't give you a chance to save your stuff. Also, open files may accumulate on your hard drive, damaging other files and potentially causing your PC to goof up wildly. Just quit normally, please.

Task

CHAPTER 2

Working the Worksheet

K now the cell...

Become one with the cell...

The basic unit of construction in a house is a brick or a 2×4 piece of lumber. The basic unit in a word-processing document is the word. The basic unit in a worksheet is the cell—a kind of rubber cubbyhole for all kinds of information, big and small. Therefore, to do anything meaningful with a worksheet, you first need to know a few basics about a cell:

✓ Like a cubbyhole, a cell has four walls. Fortunately, cells can be formatted to look prettier than your typical rubber cubbyhole.

✓ Each cell has a name, which also tells you the cell's location in the worksheet. Additionally, you can assign a new name to a cell and use that name to reference the cell.

✓ Although the majority of cells in a spreadsheet may be empty, cells can contain information, text, values, or formulas.

✓ Cells can be cut, copied, pasted, deleted, inserted, or hidden. These operations can be performed on a single cell or on a group of cells en masse.

Face it, the cell is where it happens. If you know how to find a cell and put information into it, then half the spreadsheet battle has been won. The rest is just for show. ●

TASK 1

How to Move About the Worksheet

The journey may be the reward and getting there is probably half the fun, but the point is that you want to be somewhere you're not. In a worksheet, there are times when you'll need to put information into a specific cell. To do that, you need to move about the worksheet. There are several ways to do this, from the simple and obvious to the obtuse and forgettable.

Begin

1 Use the Cursor Keys

The table in the accompanying figure shows common keys you can use to move about the spreadsheet. Since entering information into a cell is a keyboardy thing, you'll probably find these cursor key commands fairly handy.

→	Move right one cell.
←	Move left one cell.
↑	Move up one cell.
↓	Move down one cell.
Ctrl + →	Move to the right edge of the data region.
Ctrl + ←	Move to the left edge of the data region.
Ctrl + ↑	Move to the top edge of the data region.
Ctrl + ↓	Move to the bottom edge of the data region.
Home	Move to the first column in the row.
End	Used as a prefix key to move to a specific location (End, → for example).
Ctrl + Home	Move to cell A1, the first cell in the worksheet.
Ctrl + End	Move to the last cell in the worksheet (found at the last column and row where you've placed information).
Page Down	Move down one screen.
Page Up	Move up one screen.
Alt + Page Down	Move right one screen.
Alt + Page Up	Move left one screen.
Ctrl + Backspace	Return to the selected cell.

2 Use the Mouse

The mouse pointer changes to a fat plus sign when it's over any cell in the worksheet. Clicking the mouse pointer on a cell selects that cell. (You can tell a cell is selected because it is highlighted by a thick border.) To move to cell A15, for example, point the mouse at that cell and click. Use the scrollbars to navigate to cells you cannot currently see in the worksheet.

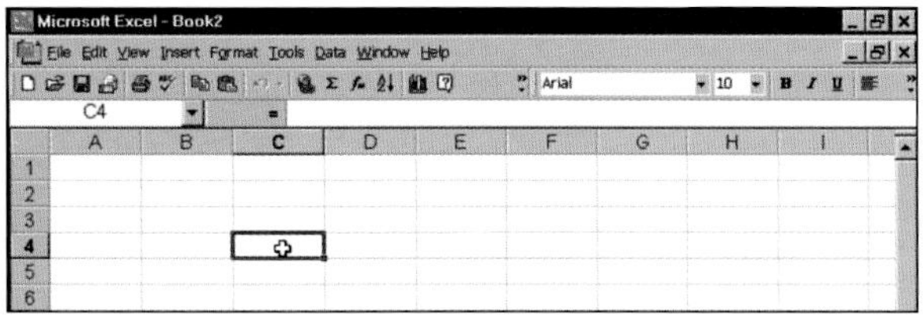

3 Type the Cell's Address

The Name box displays the column and row of the selected cell. To quickly visit a cell, type its address in the **Name** box and press **Enter**. For example, typing **W98** into the **Name** box and pressing **Enter** takes you to the cell at column W, row 98.

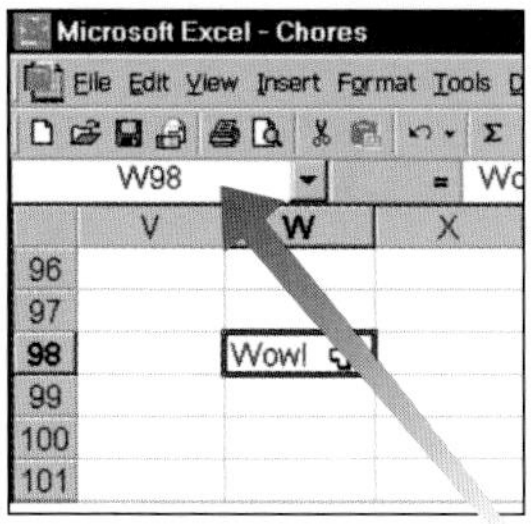

26 CHAPTER 2: WORKING THE WORKSHEET

4 Select the Cell's Name

In addition to being able to display the address of the selected cell, the Name box can list any name that has been assigned to the cell. (Naming cells is covered in Chapter 3, "Cutting, Copying, and Pasting Information.") To reach a cell that has been named, type the cell's name in the **Name** box and press **Enter**. Alternatively, click the **down arrow button** next to the **Name** box to view the drop-down list of named cells in the worksheet. Click a name in the drop-down list to select that cell.

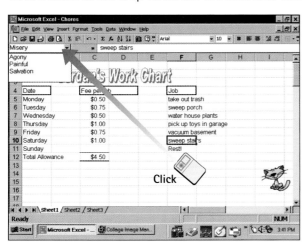

5 Use the Go To Command

You discover the world's largest spreadsheet after landing a job at General Motors. Your first task is to visit cell CZ19427. Scrollbars, anyone? Nope! Choose the **Edit** menu, then **Goto** (or press **Ctrl+G**); the Go To dialog box appears. It displays a list of cells (addresses and names) you've previously visited. Choose a cell from the list or type an address and then click **OK** to immediately go to (get it?) that cell. Click **OK**.

End

How-To Hints

The Data Region

A *data region* is any bit of filled cell space that is bordered by an empty cell. There can be several data regions in a single worksheet.

A Great Shortcut Key

Use the **Ctrl+Backspace** key combination to instantly zoom back to the selected cell(s) in your worksheet. If you've used the scrollbar to visit some other area of the worksheet, simply press **Ctrl+Backspace** to instantly return to the currently selected cell(s).

The Goto Shortcut Is Ctrl+G

I don't know how they could have made this easier: Press **Ctrl+G** to summon the Goto dialog box.

Zooming to See the Worksheet

If your worksheet is huge, use Excel's **Zoom** command to view more of the worksheet at once.

How to Enter Values and Text

Cells in a worksheet can hold three different things: values, text, or formulas. You'll use values and formulas any time you're tracking numeric data, and you'll use text for labels, headers, titles, and comments. The processes used to enter values, formulas, or text is similar, as you'll see here.

Begin

1 Select a Cell

Select the cell into which you want to place a value. You can also use the arrow keys to move to that cell. (Refer to Task 1 for more cell-plucking adventures.) If there is anything in the cell, its contents will be erased when you type in the new value.

2 Enter a Value

Type in a value and press **Enter**. (Enable your keyboard's numeric keypad for use by pressing the **Num Lock** key on your keyboard. When Num Lock is enabled, the Num Lock light on your keyboard will light up and **NUM** will appear on Excel's status bar.)

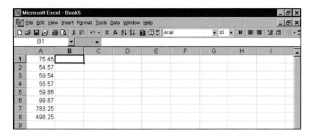

3 Enter Text

Select the cell into which you want to place text. (If the cell already contains information, that information will be replaced by the text you type.) Type some text, which can be anything—a name, heading, phone number, or symbol—and then press **Enter**. Note that when you enter a long string of text, it extends to the right of the selected cell. If the cell to the right contains an entry of its own, the extra text is hidden.

4 Multiple Lines of Text

To put more than one line of text in a cell, use the **Alt+Enter** key combination. That inserts a hard return into the cell, allowing you to enter more than one line or to break a long line so that it fits better.

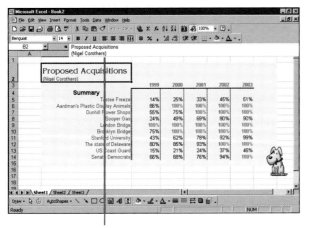

Hard Return

End

How-To Hints

Pressing the Enter Key

The Enter key can be used to signal Excel that you're done typing a value, but it's not a necessity. You can also use the arrow keys or the mouse to switch to another cell. When you do so, Excel considers the value entered.

Values Are Numbers Only

Values in a cell consist of numbers only. If there is anything else in the cell—text characters or symbols, excluding decimal points—it's not a value. Don't insert dollar signs, percent signs, or commas into the number; that's handled when you format the number (covered in Chapter 5, "Making Your Data Presentable").

Zip Codes and Phone Numbers

Even though you probably don't consider a zip code a numeric value, Excel does. This is because no symbols are used to express a zip code. Excel consider phone numbers as text, however. The dash after the prefix or the parentheses around the area code prevent Excel from seeing the number as a value. The same holds true with social security numbers and other formatted numbers.

How to Enter a Formula

Ah! The big enchilada. A worksheet filled with values and text would look pretty, but like a car without an engine, it wouldn't take you anywhere. Formulas are what churn the information in a worksheet, making it useful. Spreadsheet formulas come in varying types. At one level, covered here, the formulas can be simple math problems. At another level, formulas can be involved, complex, and can even make decisions—almost like a programming language or database. Oh, but we'll save that for a later chapter.

Begin

1 Choose the Cell

Use the mouse or arrow keys to select the cell in which you want to place the formula.

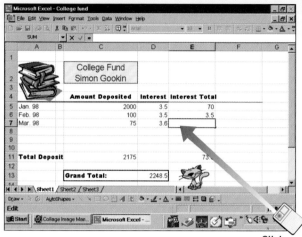

Click

2 Click the Equal Button

The Equal button is by the formula bar. This activates formula input mode.

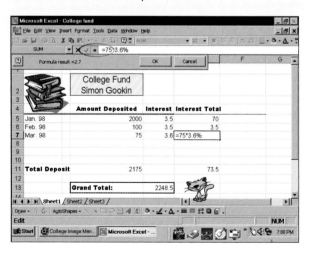

3 Enter a Formula

An OK and Cancel button appears, as does a box that displays the formula's result (the calculation) as you enter it. Simply type the formula in the text field and either click **OK** or press **Enter** to put the answer to your formula in the selected cell. (Alternatively, you can click **Cancel** or press **Esc** to cancel the formula.) Note that only the formula's result appears in the cell; the formula itself does not appear (though it's still visible on the formula bar).

4 Experiment with Formulas

The formula is basically a math problem—any old math problem. For practice, just type something such as 1+1 or 25–17. Then expand your formula to include some of the other common math operators, shown in the accompanying figure.

Symbol	Function	Sample	Result
+	Addition	2+2	4
–	Subtraction	100–25	75
–	Negation	–3	–3
*	Multiplication	4*1.25	5
/	Division	120/6	20
%	Create a percent	90%	0.9
^	Exponentiation	2^3	8
()	Groups items to work first	(1+2)*3	9

End

How-To Hints

The Equal Sign Shortcut

You can also enter a formula into a cell by typing the equal sign and then the formula. The equal sign is a shortcut, telling Excel, "This cell contains a formula, not text or a value." You may find this quicker than using the mouse and the formula bar.

Using Parentheses

Excel calculates formulas left-to-right, doing division and multiplication first and addition and subtraction second. However, if you want some part of the formula to be calculated first, surround that part with parentheses. For example, the formula 1+2*3 equals 7; Excel figures 2*3 first, then adds 1. The formula (1+2)*3 equals 9 because Excel figures 1+2 first.

The X Does Not Mean Multiply!

In school, you probably had it beaten into your brain that X means multiply (or "times"). So 4 X 4 is 16. Not so on a computer. In a worksheet, 4 X 4 is text—a four, a space, an X, a space, and a four. You use the asterisk to get 4 times 4: 4*4.

How to Reference Other Cells in a Formula

Formulas are fun. Just like playing with a calculator was fun when you were a kid, it's interesting to type in some function and have the computer come up with the answer for you. Saves time. Alas, a worksheet doesn't consist of only one cell. It's lots of cells, like lots of calculators. The most useful part of a formula is that you can reference other cells and their values and use them in your calculations.

Begin

1 Select a Cell

Use the mouse to select the cell where your formula will be. In this example, we multiply the value in cell C9 with the value in cell D9. We've selected cell E9.

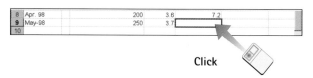

Click

2 Click the Equal Button

To multiply the values in the two other cells, start the formula by clicking the **Equal** button on the formula bar. This activates formula input mode; Excel knows the cell is to contain a formula.

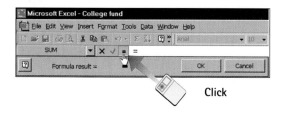

Click

3 Click the Cell with the Value

Use the mouse to choose the cell that contains the value you want; Excel then places a reference to that cell in your formula. For example, if you choose cell C9, Excel enters **C9** in the formula. (Alternatively, you can simply type a cell reference. That way you can reference cell X27 without having to scroll there and click it with the mouse.)

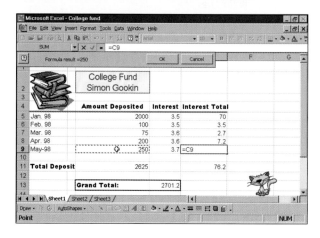

4 Type the Formula

Use any common formula function or operator. For example, to multiply the values of cells C9 and D9, you enter the formula **=C9*D9** and press **Enter**. (You can use the mouse to select the cells and the keyboard to enter the operator.) In this example, the percent sign is attached to D9 because it is literally 3.7% that you are multiplying.

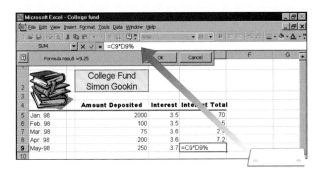

5 The Result Is Displayed

The cell you selected in step 1 contains the result of the formula you entered.

	Amount Deposited	Interest	Interest Total
Jan. 98	2000	3.5	70
Feb. 98	100	3.5	3.5
Mar. 98	75	3.6	2.7
Apr. 98	200	3.6	7.2
May-98	250	3.7	9.25

End

How-To Hints

Avoiding Complex Formulas

One way to make entering a complex formula easy is to split the formula up between several cells. For example, have one cell calculate an initial value, have the second cell subtract something from that value, and have a final cell divide the value by something else. That way you can better read and understand the function, as opposed to stuffing it all into one cell.

Various Referencing Errors

Every so often, you'll receive an error message when working with formulas. For example, the error **#REF!** means that the formula references a cell that is no longer there. Fix the formula to reference the cell's new location. The error **#VALUE!** indicates that the formula references a cell that contains text or some other improper value. The error **#DIV/0!** indicates that the formula attempts to divide by 0, which is mathematically impossible (or so they claim).

A One-on-One Reference

A formula that references another cell need not be an entire formula. For example, if you want to have the current cell simply redisplay the value in cell D5, the formula could simply be **=D5**. This is a great way to display values not visible on the screen, in another worksheet, or with a different type of formatting applied.

How to Change Data

The amazing thing about a spreadsheet is the ponderous "What if" scenario. For example, say you have a huge spreadsheet that tracks your monthly expenses. You can say, "What if I put 10% of my income into savings? How does that affect things?" Change a value from whatever to 10%, and the results are calculated instantly before your eyes. "What if" means to change, and since Excel recalculates values as fast as you can press the Enter key, seeing "what if" can be quite interesting.

Begin

1 Select the Cell

The brute-force method of changing a cell's contents is easy. The first step is to find the cell you want to change. Click the cell to select it.

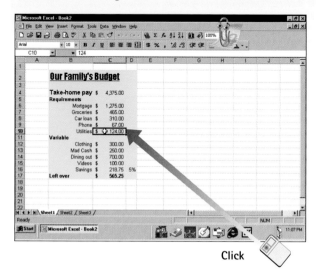

Click

2 Change Data by Retyping

Type in a new value, text, or formula. You can go back and continue changing values and formulas all over your worksheet. Just sit back and watch your worksheet change.

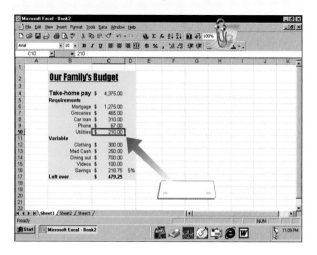

3 Press Enter

Press **Enter** after you've typed in new data. Any cells referencing that cell are updated. For example, changing the Savings value from 5% to 10% affects the Savings value as well as the Left Over value.

4 Change Data Using the F2 Key

In Excel, the F2 key is the cell editing key. Choosing a cell and pressing **F2** displays the cell's formula—right there in the cell. Any cells referenced in the formula are highlighted in the worksheet using specific colors (which is handy). Use the **arrow** keys to back up and retype, or use the **Delete** and **Backspace** keys to modify. Pressing **Enter** locks in any changes.

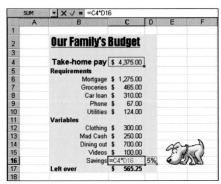

End

How-To Hints

Take Advantage of the F2 Key

When you press the **F2** key to edit a cell's formula, the cells referenced in the formula change colors. That way you can instantly track which cells are being referenced, just in case the problem with the formula is with another cell and not with the formula itself.

Use Windows Editing Keys to Edit

When you press the **F2** key, you can use Windows' standard editing keys (left arrow, right arrow, Home, End, Ctrl, and so on) to edit any text in a cell. You can even use the Shift key to select text for copying and pasting.

Don't Forget Undo!

If your editing results in havoc, you can always press **Ctrl+Z** or open the **Edit** menu and choose **Undo** to change things to the way they were before.

How to Fill Groups of Cells

One of the (granted, few) reasons to like a computer is that it can toil and sweat, doing tasks over and over without complaint. Oftentimes in a worksheet, you'll have to enter rows and columns of identical or repetitive values. Fortunately, Excel makes that easy by using the computer to do most of the dirty work. In most cases, all you need to do is create the first cell in the sequence. Then, with either a formula or mouse drag, a whole column or row can be filled with information. It's that cinchy.

Begin

1 Select a Chunk of Cells

The most efficient way to fill a group of cells is to select them and press **Ctrl+Enter**; this fills them all with the same information. To start, click the mouse and then drag it over two or more cells. They can be cells in a row or column, or a block of cells. To select a row, column, or block larger than the screen, click the **Name** box and then type the starting cell, a colon, and the ending cell.

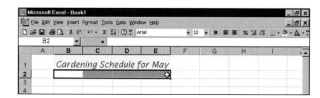

2 Fill the Cells

Enter either a bit of text or a value. Although you have a chunk of cells selected, the stuff you type appears only in the top or leftmost cell. That's okay. Pressing **Ctrl+Enter** fills all the cells with the same value. Do not click the first cell before you type. This will eliminate the whole row you selected. Just start typing. Excel will know where to put the text.

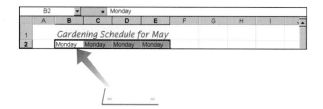

3 Drag Using the Cell's Fill Handle

Another way to fill cells with a specific value is to use a cell's fill handle. Pick a cell that already contains information (or enter the information yourself) and use the fill handle to drag the cell and its contents down or to the right. Each cell that you drag your mouse across will be filled with the same value as the original cell.

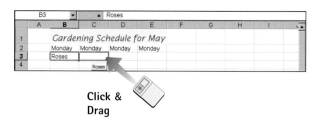

Click & Drag

4 Fill Cells with Incrementing Values

You may need to fill a group of cells with an incrementing value. For example, to create a row of years or a column numbered from 1 through whatever. To do this, begin by typing the first value in the range (usually 1) in the appropriate cell. Select the next cell (down or to the right) and enter the incrementing formula: **=previous_cell+1**. For example, since the initial cell is A3, you'd type **=A3+1**. However, the value doesn't always have to be increased by 1. For example, **=previous_cell−1** creates a decrementing list, **=previous_cell+5** creates a list that increments by values of 5, and **=previous_cell/2** creates a list that gets smaller by half for each cell. You get the idea.

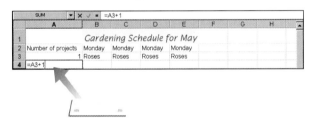

5 Drag the Cell's Fill Handle

Drag the second cell's fill handle down or to the right to create the series. Every cell you drag contains the same formula: "equals the previous cell, plus one."

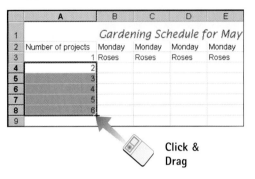

Click & Drag

6 Fill Months and Days

Here's a neat trick: Type **Monday** or **January** into a cell and use the fill handle to drag down or the right. Excel automatically continues the series as long as you drag. This is ideal for setting up calendar-related information.

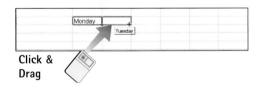

Click & Drag

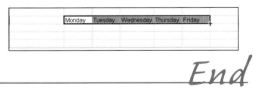

End

How-To Hints

Beware of Relative References!

Formulas in a cell reference other cells *relatively*, not *absolutely*. For example, suppose you have a column of cells filled with the value =F5. The top cell displays the value of cell F5, but the next cell down displays the value of cell F6, and the next F7 and so on. If this is what you want, fine; otherwise, use the =$F$5 (absolute) reference instead. With =$F$5, all the cells contain the value of cell F5. To reference a single cell, you need to specify it with dollar signs (**$F$1**). You get the value of cell F1 if you use just F1 (with no dollar sign). The cell reference changes if you copy or fill that formula. Drag down and the next cell becomes F2, then F3, and so on. If you want to always reference cell F1, you need to make it an absolute reference: **$F$1**.

How to Name a Range of Cells

You name your kids. You name your pets. You might even name your cars. So why not name some cells? While column letters and row numbers are fine for identifying random cells, sometimes they're just not good enough. Besides, why make yourself suffer when Excel lets you name a single cell or range of cells? You can use the name you assign to a cell or a group of cells in any formula, instead of using the cell's address, and you can type a cell's name in the Name box to instantly go to that cell.

Begin

1 Select a Chunk of Cells

Choose one cell or drag the mouse to select a range of cells that you want to name. (Yes, you can name individual cells even after you've named them in a group. You can even assign multiple names to the same cell.)

2 Click the Mouse in the Name Box

The cell's current address appears in the Name box. Click the **Name** drop-down list to select the address and type a new name for the cell(s). No spaces! The cells are named when you press **Enter**.

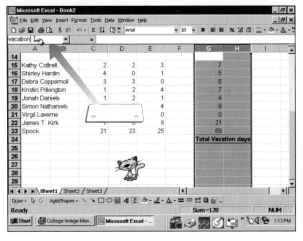

3 Use the Name Box to Visit Cells

To instantly jump to any named cell in your worksheet, click the **down arrow button** (to the right of the Name box) and then select the name of the cell you want to visit. Excel zooms you to that cell. If the name refers to a group of cells, then those cells are selected.

Click

4 Change or Delete a Name

To change or delete names in the work-sheet, open the **Insert** menu and choose **Name,** then **Define**. The Define Name dialog box appears. To change a name, click it with the mouse to select it; type the new range of cells in the **Refers To** part of the dialog box (or click the button to the right side of that box to manually select the cells). To delete a name, select the name and click the **Delete** button. Click **OK** when you're done.

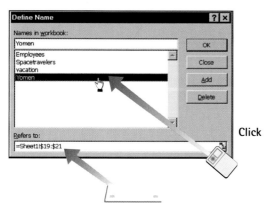

Click

End

How-To Hints

All About the Names

Excel lets you give a name to any cell providing that you use letters, numbers, periods, and underlines (_) only; you use no spaces; and no names similar to cell names, such as Z100. You can use two or more words, but separate each by an underline, as in last_week, gross_profits, or Not_for_the_IRS. Excel is not *case sensitive*; that is, it doesn't care if you use upper- or lowercase letters when typing names.

Using Names in a Formula

To use names in a formula, simply specify the name instead of the cell's address: **=income-expenses** or **=SUM(January)**, for example.

The Name Box Is Gone!

When you enter a formula, you'll notice that the Name box is replaced by the Functions drop-down list. Uh-oh. Either remember the cell names in your formula or resort to clicking the mouse on the proper cell to insert it into your formula. (Or you can just give up and play another round of FreeCell.)

How to Delete or Clear Cells, Rows, or Columns

Part of the basic cell editing and clean-up process involves the removal of cells and their contents, either by deleting or clearing them. In Excel, the word *delete* means to remove the information from a cell, while the term *clear* means removing both the information and the cell's formatting.

When it comes to destruction in Excel, there are several levels: You can delete a cell's contents or formatting, or you can just blast the entire cell's existence into smithereens, starting over with a fresh slate. The same can be done with groups of cells, rows, columns, what-have-you.

Begin

1 Delete a Cell's Contents

Select the cell(s) you want to clear out, and press the **Delete** key. This removes the cell's contents (the information displayed), but leaves the cell's formatting intact; any new information you type into the cell will retain the original's formatting.

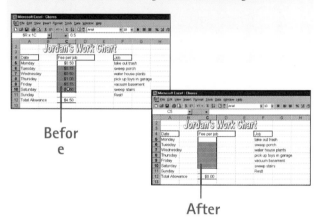

Before

After

2 Remove a Cell's Formatting

Select the cell whose formatting you want to remove. Open the Edit menu and choose **Clear, Formats**. This removes any cell formatting—font formatting, alignment, shading, colors—but retains the cell's information.

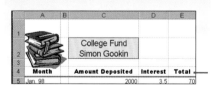

Before formatting is removed

After formatting is removed

3 Zap a Cell to Kingdom Come

To clear a cell's entire content and formatting, select the cell (or group of cells), open the **Edit** menu, choose **Clear**, and select **All**. This leaves you with essentially the same empty cell(s) you had when you started the worksheet. To clear a cell's entire content, select the cell (or group of cells), open the **Edit** menu and choose **Clear, All**.

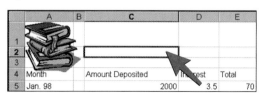

4 Remove an Entire Row

Click the row number along the left side of the window to select the row you want to delete (or click and drag over several rows to select them all). The row disappears when you open the **Edit** menu and choose **Delete**. Notice that the information in subsequent rows moves up, filling in the row you deleted, and that the remaining rows renumber themselves.

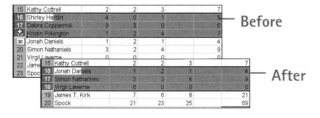

Before

After

5 Remove an Entire Column

Either click a column heading to select that column or drag over several column headings to select them all. Open the **Edit** menu and choose **Delete**. The column disappears, smooshing everything to the right.

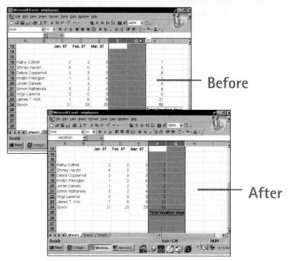

Before

After

End

<hr />

How-To Hints

Deleting the Whole Worksheet

If you're frustrated and want to start over with your whole worksheet, select all the cells in a worksheet by choosing **Select All** from the **Edit** menu (or typing **Ctrl+A**). Open the **Edit** menu and choose **Clear, All**.

Comments in Cells?

If you open the **Edit** menu and choose **Clear**, you'll notice that one of the options in the Clear submenu is Comments. To add a comment to a cell, open the **Insert** menu, choose **Comment**, and type the comment in a cartoon bubble by the cell. That commented cell then has a red triangle in its upper-right corner; pointing the mouse at the red triangle displays the cell's comment. Of course, you can delete the comment by opening the **Edit** menu and choosing **Clear, Comment**.

TASK 9

How to Hide Rows or Columns

Just because you have information on a spreadsheet doesn't mean you need to have it all on display. You may want to hide information, such as the total dollar amount you spend on shoes per year. Or maybe you just want to hide a part of the spreadsheet that contains trivial matter so that your boss can see the Big Picture. There are several ways to hide and display information in Excel, some obvious and handy, others very cute and interesting.

Begin

1 Hide Rows

Select one or more rows, open the **Format** menu, and choose **Row**, **Hide**.

Click

2 The Rows Are Hidden

The rows disappear! Your big clue that something is hidden (as opposed to deleted) is that the row numbers are no longer in order.

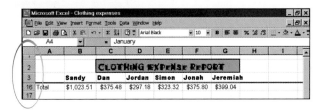

3 Hide Columns

Hiding columns works much like hiding rows: Select one or more columns to hide, open the **Format** menu, choose **Column** (instead of **Row**), and select **Hide**. The columns are hidden from view; their missing letters are your only clue that they're gone.

Clicking a row or column header with the right mouse button displays a shortcut menu containing the Hide command.

OK

4 Display Rows or Columns

Displaying rows and columns is mysterious. Select the first row or column before the missing bunch and drag over to the row or column after the missing bunch. Open the **Format** menu, choose **Row** or **Column** (depending on what you're displaying), and select **Unhide** to make the invisible visible once again.

Click

5 Grouping Rows or Columns

Another way to hide rows or columns is to pull them into a group, which is displayed either to the left or on top of your spreadsheet. Select a group of rows or columns by clicking their headers (or drag over the headers with the mouse). Open the **Data** menu, choose **Group and Outline**, and click **Group.** This collects the rows or columns as a group and displays a new left side or top above the columns. To remove the group, select the whole group that was originally selected, open the **Data** menu, choose **Group and Outline**, and select **Ungroup**.

	A	B	G	H
11				
12				
13				
14				
15	Kathy Cottrell		7	
16	Shirley Hardin		5	
17	Debra Coppernoll		6	
18	Kristin Pilkington		7	
19	Jonah Daniels		4	
20	Simon Nathaniels		9	
21	Virgil Laverne		0	
22	James T. Kirk		21	
23	Spock		69	
24			**Total Vacation days**	

End

How-To Hints

The Right-Click Shortcut

To quickly hide any row, column, or group, right-click the row or column heading and choose **Hide** from the pop-up menu.

More Groups!

You can create subgroups inside any row or column groups you create. Just select a stack of rows or bunch of columns inside the group, open the **Data** menu, choose **Group and Outline**, and click **Group**.

How to Insert or Remove Cells

Taking the family picture is tough. The poor waitress keeps backing up and up. Cousin Lloyd is too tall and Aunt Debra is too far to the left, so someone says, "Everyone move left," and she just keeps moving left. . .

Fortunately, Excel easily lets you move things around. You can inch, skootch, or nudge cells over or under to make room for more. You can also zap specific cells to the netherworld just like picking grapes. The rest of the cells in the worksheet graciously move over or under to make room. It's all very civilized.

Begin

1 Select the New Area

Tell Excel where to insert the new cell(s) by selecting one or more cells. Open the **Insert** menu and choose **Cells**.

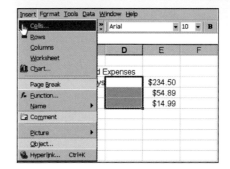

2 Shift Cells Down or to the Right

In the Insert dialog box, decide whether you want existing cells to be shoved to the right or down. Choose the appropriate option; click **OK**. The existing cells in the worksheet slide in the proper direction, making room for your new swath of cells.

Click

3 Delete Cells

Select a single cell or drag over a group of cells to select them as a block. These are the cells you want to delete. Select the **Edit** menu, then **Delete**.

Click

4 Shift Cells Up or to the Left

The Delete dialog box appears and offers two options: shifting from the left or upward to fill in the place where you're deleting cells. Choose one and click **OK**.

Click

End

How-To Hints

The Right-Click Shortcut

Right-click the mouse on any single cell or selected group of cells and choose **Insert** or **Delete** from the pop-up menu to insert or delete cells.

To Shove Cells Right or Down?

Always try to move cells to an unused part of the spreadsheet. If you're inserting a block of cells on the right edge, choose the **Shift Cells Right** option in the Insert dialog box.

Deleting Without Moving

Remember that you can always use the **Delete** key to remove a cell's contents without shifting the rest of the cells in a worksheet up, left, or whatever. Refer to Task 8 for more detailed information.

How to Insert Rows or Columns

Some people are planners and know exactly how things are going to be before they get started. If that's you, you don't need to read this task. Most of us, however, could use a break. Excel gives you just such a break in that it lets you insert rows or columns after you've started a worksheet. Why? Because you didn't plan ahead. Of course, there's always that school of thought that says information always changes and you can't predict everything. But then there's the old saying, "There's never time enough to do it right but always time to do it over."

Begin

1 Click the Row or Column

Select the entire row or column. Excel adds the new row above the selected row number or to the left of the selected column.

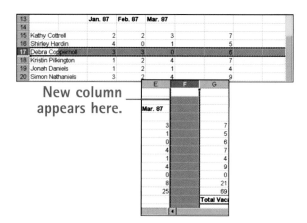

New column appears here.

2 Choose Row or Column

Open the **Insert** menu and choose **Row** or **Column**. The new row or column is added. Everything else in the spreadsheet moves over to accommodate the new guy.

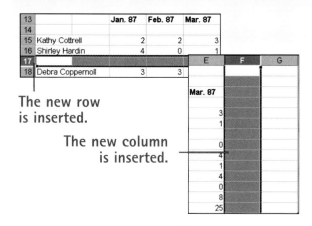

The new row is inserted.

The new column is inserted.

3 Select Either a Row or Column

To add a row or column after any cell in the worksheet, click that cell using the right mouse button. Choose **Insert** from the pop-up menu. From the Insert dialog box, you can then choose whether to insert an entire new row or column.

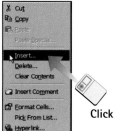

Click

Click

4 Adding Multiple Rows or Columns

Excel doesn't limit you to adding one row or column at a time. To add multiple rows or columns, select the number of rows or columns you want to add immediately below where you want it added. Then open the **Insert** menu and choose **Rows** or **Columns** to add that many rows.

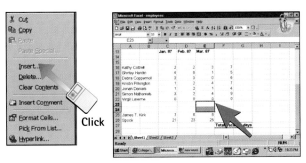

Click

End

How-To Hints

Updating Automatically

Adding rows or columns doesn't change the formulas in your worksheet. It just moves them either up or to the left and automatically updates them to reflect their new position.

Task

Cutting, Copying, and Pasting Information

'll bet when you were in kindergarten learning to cut and paste you weren't aware that you were being taught valuable computer skills. It's true. Moving or copying information hither, thither, and yon is what makes a computer so powerful and, ultimately, useful. And it's not only cut-and-paste skills that are important, but copying and pasting as well. (Of course, I seriously doubt whether allowing kindergartners to use photocopier machines is such a great idea—and besides, I would question the school's motives.)

No—cutting, copying, and pasting are all part of the computer world, just like inserting French words into normally readable text is part of a writer's world.

In Excel, as in all of Windows, *cut and paste* means moving information. You cut it from here, paste it over there—a move. Nothing exotic there. Copying information is done by copy and paste. The original information stays put, but a duplicate is pasted over there—a copy. Simple enough. The information cut or copied is stored in Windows' (not Excel's) Clipboard. From there, it can be pasted again and again, back into the worksheet dozens of times if you like.

A new feature with Excel 2000 is the capability to *collect and paste*. Unlike normal copy and paste, Excel keeps multiple copies of what you copy when you collect and paste. (Normally Windows' Clipboard can hold only one item at a time.) ●

How to Select Cells

Before you can copy or cut information in your worksheet, you need to select one or more cells. Yeah, I know: silly. You've probably become a master of selecting cells by now. Then again, this could be your first selection, or maybe you're curious about selecting nonadjacent cells. Whatever the motivation, welcome to cell selection nirvana.

Begin

1 Select a Single Cell

Clicking the mouse on any cell selects that cell. The cell's name appears in the name box, and the cell has a black border around it.

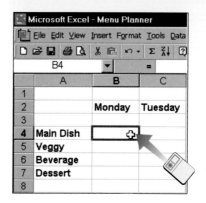

Click

2 Select Multiple Cells

Click and drag the mouse down, up, or over to select a chunk of cells. Cells can be selected in a row, in a column, or as a block.

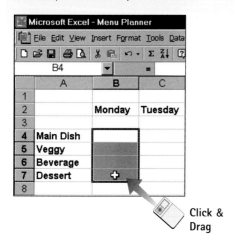

Click & Drag

3 Select Cells Using the Name Box

Click the **Name** box to activate it and then type the address of the first cell, a colon, and the address of the last cell. For example, to select the first 10 cells in column A, type **A1:A10**.

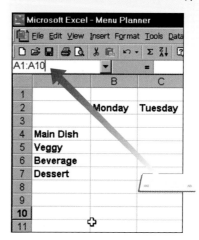

4 Select Random Cells

Your cell selections need not be contiguous. To select a group of cells without dragging the mouse, use the **Ctrl** key. As long as you keep the Ctrl key held down, clicking or dragging the mouse continues to select cells. Any action you then perform (formatting, clearing, naming) affects all the selected cells.

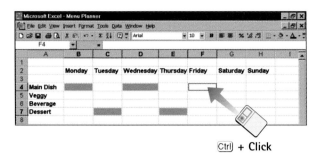

Ctrl + Click

5 Select a Range of Cells

You can select a group of cells by clicking a cell in the corner of the group, holding down the **Shift** key, and then clicking the opposite corner of the group. This nifty little step is call *Shift-clicking.*

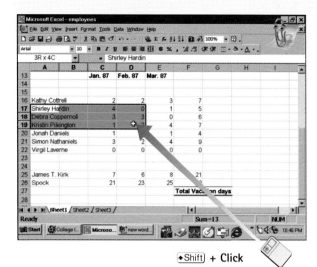

◆Shift + Click

End

How-To Hints

Selecting More Cells Than You See

If you need to select a large swath of cells, use the Name box as opposed to dragging the mouse. For example, type **A1:CV1** to select the first 100 cells in row 1. This is much easier than dragging the mouse.

Trouble with Ctrl+Click?

If you need to select random cells, start by selecting the first cell without holding down the Ctrl key. Then hold down the **Ctrl** key as you select additional cells. You can release the Ctrl key when you're done selecting cells.

What? Can't Copy or Cut?

Excel will not let you copy or cut multiple selections (that is, selections made with **Ctrl+click**). Sorry! See Task 4 on collecting and pasting.

How to Copy and Paste Cells

Copying, the awkward way: Wheel that 10,000-pound photocopier just in front of your PC. Now tilt the monitor down so that it's face is against the glass in the photocopier. Press the green button. Soon a copy of the worksheet appears in the photocopier's out bin.

Copying, the best way: Select the cell(s) you want to copy, copy them, and pick out a spot in which to paste them. Easy as cake.

Begin

1 Select the Cell(s)

Either click the cells you want to copy with the mouse or drag over them to select more than one. (See Task 1 for more information about selecting cells.)

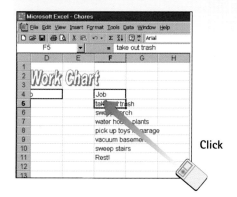

Click

2 Copy the Cells

Choose **Copy** from the **Edit** menu. After the cells are copied, you'll see the selected originals appear bordered with a line of *marching ants*. That's your visual clue that the cells have been copied and are now awaiting pasting.

Click

3 Choose the Cell in Which to Paste

Click the cell in which you want to paste the copy. You'll notice that the marching ants continue to march (if you can see those cells on the screen). There is no need to select an area equal in size to the cells you're copying. (Thank goodness, and it's about time.)

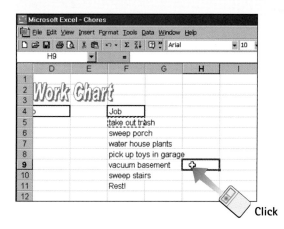

Click

4 Paste the Cells

Choose **Paste** from the **Edit** menu. The cells are pasted exactly as copied. They will replace, or paste over, any cells already in the worksheet. Press **Enter** to stop the marching ants from moving around your selected cell.

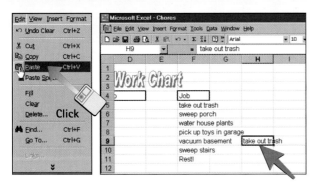

5 Toolbar Icons

There are toolbar icons for copying and pasting as well. The Copy button has two sheets of paper on it (common to most Windows programs), and the Paste button looks like a tiny clipboard.

End

How-To Hints

Keyboard Shortcuts You Should Know

The keyboard shortcut for copying is **Ctrl+C**. Easy; the shortcut key for pasting is **Ctrl+V**.

And the ######## Thing Is What?

When you paste in cells, you may notice that some of the values read as **########**. That's Excel's way of telling you that the value is too wide for the cell. See Chapter 6, "Sprucing Up the Worksheet," for information on adjusting column width.

My Formulas Are Screwed Up!

Pasting a formula does not automatically update the formula's references. You may notice a **#REF!** or **#DIV/0!** error when you paste a group of cells; or you may notice merely a blank value. That means the formula doesn't reference the proper cells. You either have to delete the cells or edit them to point at the proper cells. See Chapter 2, "Working the Worksheet," for information on editing a cell's value.

I Can't Re-Paste!

The marching ants, signifying the cells you selected and copied, march until you perform some fatalistic act: entering a new formula, editing a cell, deleting a cell, and so on. These actions turn off the marching ants. Can't re-paste what you just copied? In Excel, unlike other Windows programs, you can only paste while those cells you're copying are surrounded by the marching ants. When they are gone, Excel no longer lets you re-paste the information.

How to Cut and Paste Cells

Cutting, the bad way: Moving cells in your worksheet can be easy, provided you have the proper electrical and glass-working skills. First, use a glass cutter to remove the section of cells you see on the monitor. Be careful: The monitor's insides are a vacuum and the wires in the yoke hold close to 14,000 volts.

Cutting, the easy way: Selecting cells and moving them hither and thither is easy in Excel. A drag of the mouse, a few swift keystrokes (or a menu command), and the cells are gone from here and pasted over there. No paper cuts.

Begin

1 Select the Cell You Yearn to Cut

Either use the mouse to select one cell or drag to select a row, column, or group of cells. (Refer to Task 1 for more information about selecting cells.)

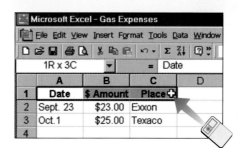

Click & Drag

2 Cut the Cells

Choose the **Edit** menu, then **Cut**. Hey! The cells are still there! Actually, they're waiting to be pasted; the cells aren't moved until you paste. Until then, they are surrounded by a protective barrier of marching ants.

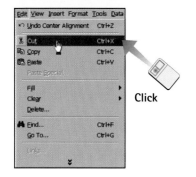

Click

3 Choose the Cell in Which to Paste

Click the cell in which you want to paste the cut cells. If you're pasting in a block of cells, the cell you select marks the upper-left corner of the block; any cells already containing information will be overwritten by the cells you paste.

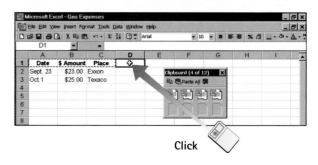

Click

4 Paste the Cells

Choose the **Edit** menu, then **Paste** to move the cut cells to the selected location.

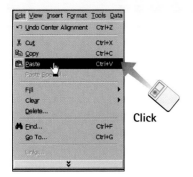

Click

5 The Cells Are Moved

The cells are moved to their new location. You'll notice that the line of ants and original cells are now gone.

End

How-To Hints

Keyboard Cutting Shortcuts

The keyboard shortcut for cutting is **Ctrl+X**, where the X probably means "cut" (though I tend to think of the X as a pair of scissors). The shortcut key for pasting is **Ctrl+V**—V as in paste.

Toolbar Buttons for Cut and Paste

The toolbar button for cutting selected cells is the one with scissors. The toolbar icon for pasting is the wee Clipboard.

What's This Clipboard Box?

If you cut and paste and then use the Cut or Copy command again, you may see the Clipboard dialog box displayed. See Task 4 on collecting and pasting for more information.

How to Collect and Paste Cells

Collecting and pasting is something new to Excel—and to many Office 2000 applications. In reality apparently, people like you and I complained long and loud enough that Microsoft finally listened: It's redundant to have to select-copy-paste over and over again. The collect and paste feature allows you to copy (or cut) chunks of a worksheet, collecting them in a special Clipboard. From that Clipboard, you can paste a specific piece of information, several pieces, or everything you've cut or copied. A handy tool.

Begin

1 Copy or Cut a Cell or Cells

Select the cells you want to copy or cut and choose **Copy** or **Cut** from the **Edit** menu. (Refer to Task 2 for more information about copying, to Task 3 for information about cutting.) Whether you use the cut function or the copy function, the idea is to place the cells on the Clipboard.

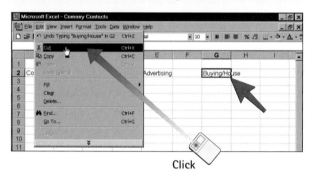

Click

2 Copy or Cut Another Cell or Cells

Before you paste the cell or cells you copied or cut in step 1, copy or cut another cell or group of cells. The second time you copy or cut, the Clipboard dialog box appears. It can contain up to 12 "scrap" icons representing chunks of the worksheet you've recently cut or copied. You can point the mouse at a scrap to see its contents displayed in a bubble beneath it.

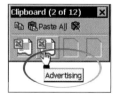

3 Click a Scrap Icon

You can choose any scrap icon in any order; click one after the other if you want to paste several different items. Note that you can click to select cells in the worksheet even as you paste from the Clipboard dialog box; the Clipboard dialog box stays open until you close it. Use the **Paste All** button to paste in every item all at once.

Click

4 Close the Clipboard Window

If you want to clear the Clipboard dialog box, click the icon in the dialog box that looks like a clipboard with a × over it. Click the × button in the upper-right corner of the window to close it when you're done.

Click

End

How-To Hints

Adding a Specific Scrap

To add a specific group of cells to the Clipboard dialog box, make sure the dialog box is open, select the cells you want to add, and then click the **Copy** button in the dialog box. The cells' information is added as a scrap icon.

Viewing the Clipboard Dialog Box

You can view the Clipboard dialog box at any time. Simply open the **View** menu and choose **Toolbars, Clipboard**.

How to Drag Cells Around the Worksheet

Copying or moving cells can be a real drag—literally. Providing you want to move or copy a chunk of cells somewhere you can see on the screen, you can use the mouse to copy or move the cells. (I say "see on the screen" because dragging with the mouse can be unwieldly if you have to drag and scroll at the same time.) This isn't really a new feature; Windows has had the capability to drag and copy or move file icons for a few years now. It's just yet another way of doing things in Excel—a handy way if you just need to nudge some cells over a row or column.

Begin

1 Select Cells You Want to Move

You can select one cell with the mouse or an entire swath by dragging the mouse. (The cells must be a block, not selected by **Ctrl+click** with the mouse.)

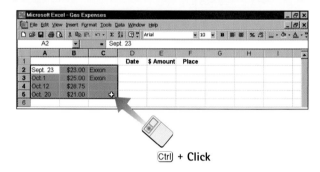

Ctrl + **Click**

2 Point the Mouse and Drag

Point the mouse at the heavy border surrounding the selected cell(s). When you find the sweet spot, the mouse pointer changes to an arrow instead of a fat plus sign. Drag the cell or group of cells to a new location. If the cells in the new location contain any information, you are asked if you want to replace it with the new information.

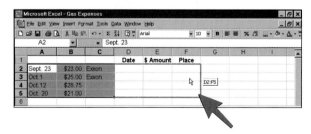

3 Select a Group to Copy

Select one cell or a group of cells that you want to copy. (Again, the cells can't be selected by **Ctrl+click**.)

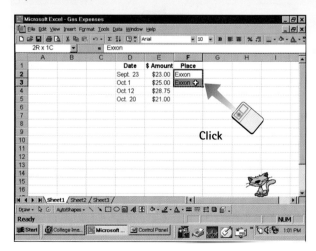

Click

4 Use the Mouse and Ctrl Key

Press and hold down the **Ctrl** key; use the mouse to **Ctrl+drag** the cell(s). When you press the Ctrl key, the mouse pointer grows a plus sign by its arrow. That's your clue that the cells you drag around are being copied, not moved.

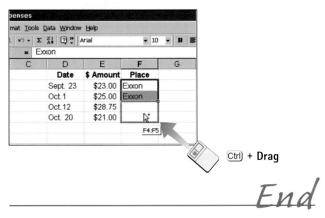

Ctrl + Drag

End

How-To Hints

Using the Right Drag

If you drag the cells using the right mouse button, a pop-up menu appears when you release the button. From the menu, you can select whether you want to move, copy, or even insert the cells into their new location.

No Re-Pasting?

The cells you drag are not officially copied or pasted, so you cannot use the Clipboard to re-paste them, nor can you use the collect-and-paste Clipboard to see their values.

Dragging Outside the Screen

This drag-move and drag-copy operation works best if you're moving or copying cells to a spot you can see. Otherwise, you have to drag the cell and scroll the worksheet at the same time. Instead of dragging the cells, use the standard **Copy** or **Cut** commands, which are covered earlier in this chapter.

Task

4

Crunching Numbers

*H*ey, kids! It's time for the scary math stuff! Now please, *please*, remain calm. Sit down. Don't say, "This is a great time for me to find a good cup of coffee...in Seattle." Although a spreadsheet is all about numbers, please keep the following thought dangling at the top of your head: It's the *computer* that does the math.

As an example, take all those rocket scientists who send spaceships and satellites to Mars. Do you think they calculate those figures in their head, eyes up and tongue out? Probably not. Most of the old-time eggheads used slide rules as a sort of mathematical crutch. Then they went to calculators. Today they use computers. The difference between them and you? They know what formulas to enter.

Formulas are the key to getting anything done in math. Some of the real brainy folk will even tell you that mathematics is the *universal language*. (Universal for what, however, is questionable; I really don't want to be around to hear Shakespeare translated into math.) For example, you can describe a circle as a simple math formula. Of course, until you know that formula $(X^2 + Y^2 = R^2)$, figuring out how to express it is a pain.

The formulas you enter into Excel probably won't be complex to the degree required to send a rocket to Mars—unless it's Mars, Pennsylvania, and you live in Pittsburgh. Still, Excel does have an armada of formulas, plus various helpers and whatnot to assist you should you need more information. All you need to know is which goal you need to meet. Excel does the rest.

The most common spreadsheet formula is SUM. It calculates the result of adding all the cells in a row, column, or group (and it saves wear and tear on the + key). Other functions perform common calculations, adjust values, compare numbers, and do everything from finding the average of some cells to figuring out an interest payment on a loan. (And, yes, you can even calculate escape velocity, though there isn't really a specific Excel formula for that.) ●

How to Use the SUM Function

The SUM function is the most popular spreadsheet function of all time. It takes a column or row of numbers and totals them—something that happens more often than you would think in a spreadsheet. In hyper mode, the SUM function calculates the result of not just a column or row, but any block or random collection of cells. All you do is specify the range of cells or individual cells (or both); the SUM function does the rest. It's an amazing tool.

Begin

1 Select the Cell

Select the cell where the result of the SUM function will be placed. The cell could be anywhere, though it's traditionally located at the bottom of a column of numbers or to the right of a row of numbers.

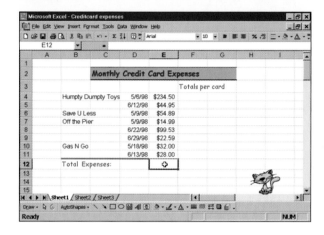

2 Click the Equal Button

Once you click the **Equal** button, Excel goes into function mode. Notice that the **Name** box now contains a drop-down list of functions. If you're lucky, the SUM function is listed there already, at the top.

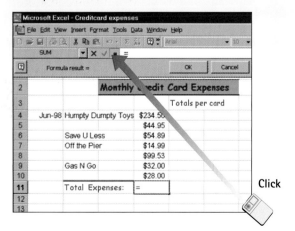

Click

3 Choose the SUM Function

Click the **SUM** function in the **Name** box. You may have to click the down arrow to display the list. If the SUM function isn't in the list, choose **More Functions** from the bottom of the list to display the Paste Function dialog box. Choose **Math & Trig** from the **Function** category and choose **SUM** from the **Function** name list. Click **OK**; the function is pasted into the cell and the result displayed.

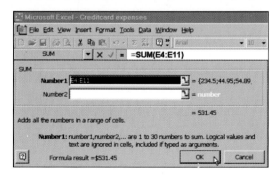

4 Click the SUM Button

The AutoSUM button smartly figures out which cells you most likely want to total and automatically selects them in the formula. If that's what you want, click the **AutoSUM** button and then press the **Enter** key. Otherwise, use the mouse to select the group of cells you want totaled and then press the **Enter** key.

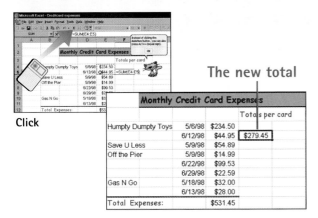

Click

The new total

Monthly Credit Card Expenses			
			Totals per card
Humpty Dumpty Toys	5/6/98	$234.50	
	6/12/98	$44.95	$279.45
Save U Less	5/9/98	$54.89	
Off the Pier	5/9/98	$14.99	
	6/22/98	$99.53	
	6/29/98	$22.59	
Gas N Go	5/18/98	$32.00	
	6/13/98	$28.00	
Total Expenses:		$531.45	

5 Select a Hodgepodge of Cells

To total cells from all over, select a cell and click the **SUM** button on the toolbar. Then press and hold the **Ctrl** key and use the mouse to click cells to total. Excel marks all the cells you select with the marching ants, and the cells' addresses are placed between the parentheses in the SUM function formula. Press the **Enter** key to lock in the formula.

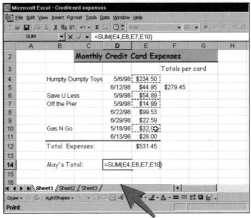

End

How-To Hints

Choose More Cells to Total

If you want to add more cells to the total, press the **Tab** key in the SUM function dialog box to add those cells. You can repeat the step as often as necessary to continue adding cells to the SUM function. Note how Excel stores the cells in the function; all the cells to be totaled appear in parentheses after the SUM function name.

Multiple Functions? No Way!

The SUM function can be used by itself or with other functions. For example, you may need to calculate the total of a row of cells and then multiply it by 4: =SUM(C5:C7)*4. Use the SUM function as described in this task, but then enter the rest of the formula (the *4 part) before pressing the **Enter** key.

Total Columns and Rows

Here's a handy trick: Suppose you have a chunk of numbers, a block of rows and columns. To quickly get the sum of all rows and columns, select the block—but also select the next cell down and over. Click the **SUM** button on the toolbar. Excel calculates the sum of all columns and rows and then the sum of the totals. Nifty.

How to Paste in a Formula

In Excel, it's not knowing the formula that's important, but knowing which formula to use. Once you find the formula you need, all you need to do is paste it into your worksheet. No matter what formula you're using, the steps for pasting it into a worksheet are similar; so instead of showing you *every* formula that Excel offers (and making this book eight inches thick), we'll just stick to one example: the PMT function used to calculate a loan.

Begin

1 Enter Values for a Loan Payment

Enter the total amount of the loan (the outstanding balance), the term of the loan (how long until it's paid off, listed as months or years), and the interest rate (as a percentage). Then click the cell in which you want to paste the function.

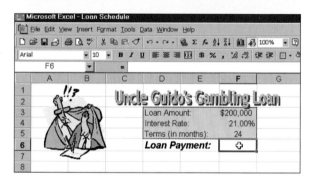

2 Paste the Function

Click the **Paste Function** toolbar button to open the Paste Function dialog. Functions are grouped by category, with the categories appearing on the left and the functions appearing on the right. The PMT function is a financial function, so click **Financial** in the left pane and select **PMT** in the right pane. A description of the PMT function appears in the bottom part of the dialog box. Click **OK**.

Click

3 Enter the Interest Rate

The PMT dialog box appears, ready for you to fill in the blanks. (If the dialog box has a scrollbar, remember to use it to fill in any blanks not immediately visible.) To enter the interest rate, click in the **Rate** text field and then click the cell in the worksheet that contains the interest rate value. (Note that the cell address, rather than the value itself, is what appears in the field.) Type **/12** to divide the rate by 12. (You want the monthly interest rate if you're calculating a monthly interest payment.)

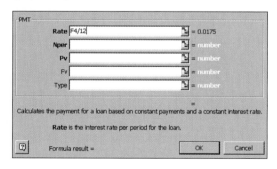

4 Enter the Nper Value

Enter the address of the cell that contains the Nper (number of periods) value, which tells the PMT formula how many payments you'll make on the loan (the term or length of the loan). As before, you want this term in the number of months.

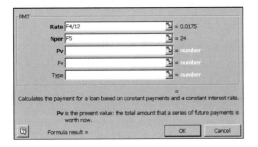

5 The Pv Value

The Pv value is the current outstanding balance—the present value of the loan. Here's a trick: press the minus key before clicking the cell containing the outstanding balance. This automatically changes what would ordinarily be a negative value into a positive one. (It is easier to work with and understand positive amounts of money.) There's no need to divide or multiply by a monthly value here because you're dealing with the entire outstanding value.

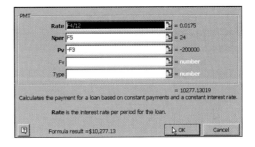

6 View the Result of the Function

Click **OK** once you've filled in all the required text fields (those whose names are in bold) in the Function dialog box (along with any of the fields that aren't required by Excel, but that may be required by you). The function is pasted into the worksheet and the result is displayed.

End

How-To Hints

Using the Name Box

When you press the equal key to begin a function, the Name box changes to a drop-down list of recently used functions. If your function is among them, pluck it from the list to display the function's dialog box.

Are You Nuts?

You can click the **Equal** button on the formula bar and type a function name to open the function's dialog box. This is useful if you know the function's name but aren't quite insane enough to remember all the required values.

A Better Way to Edit a Formula

Select the cell containing the formula and click the equal button to redisplay the formula's dialog box, ready for editing.

How to Use the IF Formula

In addition to just spewing out values, a formula can also be used to make decisions. For example, you may have a worksheet that calculates your payments on a bank card: If the amount you owe is below $20, then the bank charges you the $20 minimum anyway. This is an IF-type of decision: "If the value is less than $20, then charge $20 anyway."

The IF formula compares values and displays other values or formulas as a result. Alas, the IF function cannot make overly complex decisions. For example, it can't decide when to paint the house or whether Barbara is really in love with Steve. But it comes close!

Begin

1 Choose the IF Function Cell

Select the cell where the IF function will go. Use your mouse or hunt the cell down by viciously whacking an arrow key.

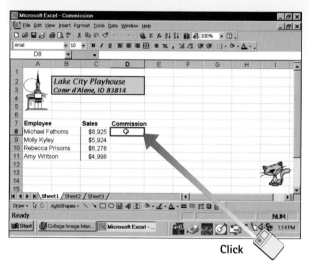

Click

2 Choose the IF Function

Either choose **Function** from the **Insert** menu or click the **Paste Function** button on the toolbar. In the Paste Function dialog box, choose **Logical** from the **Function Category** first; then choose **IF** from the **Function name** list. Click **OK**.

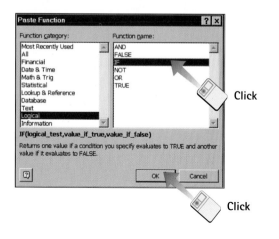

Click

Click

3 Fill in the Logical_Test Field

The IF function must compare two cells or values to get a true or false result. There are several operators you can use to compare cells or values: = (equals), > (greater than), < (less than), >= (greater than or equal to), <= (less than or equal to), and <> (not equal). As an example, suppose the value of cell C8 has to be more than $5,000 for an employee to get a commission; the equation would be **C8>5000**. The IF function then determines if this condition is true or false.

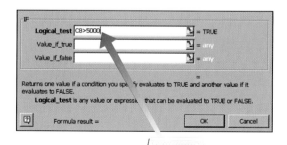

4 Fill in the Value_If_True Field

When the condition in the Logical_Test field is true, the value you enter in Value_If_True field is displayed on the worksheet. It can be the value of another cell, a specific value, or even a string of text you type in. Using the previous example, if C8>5000, then the result of the formula entered in the Value_If_True field (in this case, **C8*10%**—10% commission) is displayed on the worksheet.

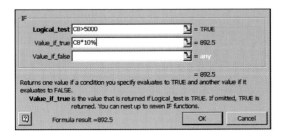

5 Fill in the Value_If_False Field

When the condition in the Logical_Test field is false, the value entered in the Value_If_False field is displayed on the worksheet. You can enter a cell address, a value, or a text string in this field. Again using the previous example, if C8<5000 is false, then the result of the formula entered in the Value_If_False field (**C8*2%**—2% commission) is displayed on the worksheet.

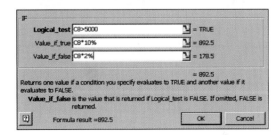

6 Paste the Function

Click **OK** in the IF dialog box; Excel calculates the result and displays it in the worksheet. Note that this figure shows that the formula has been applied to several cells; refer to Chapter 2, Task 6 for information on filling in cells with the same formula.

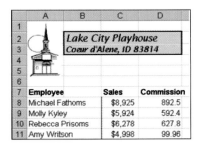

End

How-To Hints

More Functions Inside Functions

The Value_If_True and Value_If_False parts of the IF function can also contain other functions. For example, the Value_If_False value could be SUM(A1:A16), in which case that total would be displayed when the IF comparison is false.

Say the Comparison Out Loud

It helps if you read the logical test part of the IF function out loud, as in "if the value of cell D8 is less than 5,000." The IF dialog box actually displays the words **true** or **false**, helping you understand which decision is being made.

How to Round Numbers

Rounding is a fun mathematical concept that almost everyone enjoys. Why? Because it's easy and it makes working with numbers easy. When you round, you're taking a heavy number like 125,987.35 and turning it into 126,000 or even 100,000—much easier numbers to work with. Goodbye, excess number crud!

Begin

1 Choose a Cell

In Excel, you can control the degree to which things are rounded using the ROUND function. Begin by choosing a cell into which you want to paste the ROUND function.

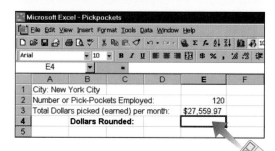

Click

2 Paste the ROUND Function

Open the Paste Function dialog box by either clicking the **Insert** menu, then choosing **Function**, or clicking the **Paste Function** tool. Choose the **Math & Trig** category and then select the **ROUND** function. Click **OK**.

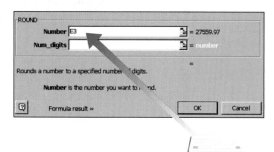

3 Type the Number You Want to Round

In the **Number** part of the ROUND dialog box, specify the value you want to round by entering its cell address or clicking the cell in the worksheet. Press the **Tab** key to move to the next box.

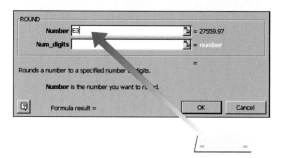

4 Enter the Number of Digits

Enter the number of digits to which you want to round the number. For example, type **-3** to round the value to the third digit (the 100s place). Typing negative numbers rounds to the left of the decimal place. Positive numbers (1, 2, 3) round to the right of the decimal. Since the dialog box displays the result, type in both negative and positive numbers to see how it affects the value. Remember to keep the numbers small (–3, –2 –1, 1, 2, 3) for smaller values. Otherwise, this process doesn't work.

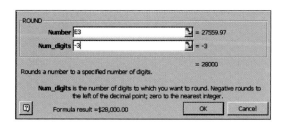

5 View the Rounded Value

Click **OK**; the rounded value appears in the spreadsheet.

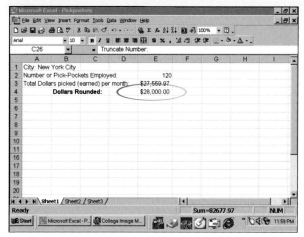

End

How-To Hints

Rounding Up or Down

The ROUND function rounds numbers up or down depending on how close they are to the nearest acceptable value. For example, 1.11 is rounded down to 1.00, and 1.89 is rounded up to 2.00.

Rounding Down All the Time

To always round values down, use the ROUNDDOWN function instead of ROUND. The values will always be rounded down. Unlike the INT function, you can use ROUNDDOWN to round down fractions (the decimal part of a number).

Rounding Up All the Time

To always round values up, use the ROUNDUP function.

Shifting the Decimal Place

There are two buttons on the toolbar that don't affect a number's value but do affect how much of a number's decimal portion is displayed. The Increase Decimal and Decrease Decimal buttons can be used to force Excel to display more or less of a value's decimal part. This doesn't affect the value, merely how the value appears in the cell.

How to Truncate Numbers

When you truncate, you're taking a knife to a number and lopping off the decimal part: 13.352 gets whacked to humble 13. Other similar concepts include INT, which transforms a complex decimal number into a whole number (similar to truncating) and ABS, which translates negative numbers into positive—an accountant's dream!

Begin

1 Paste the TRUNC Function

You use the TRUNC function to truncate a value. Begin by choosing a cell into which you want to paste the TRUNC function. Then choose **Insert, Function**. Alternatively, you can click the **Paste Function** tool. Choose the **Math & Trig** category and then select the **TRUNC** function. Click **OK**.

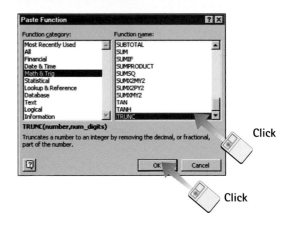

Click

Click

2 Specify a Value

The TRUNC function's dialog box is similar to the ROUND function's. However, with TRUNC you're merely lopping off values from a number—the values to the right of the decimal place are replaced with zeros. In the **Number** part of the TRUNC dialog box, specify the value you want to truncate by entering its cell address or clicking the cell in the worksheet.

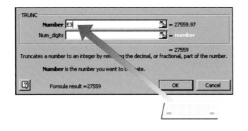

3 View the Truncated Value

Click **OK**; the truncated value appears in the spreadsheet.

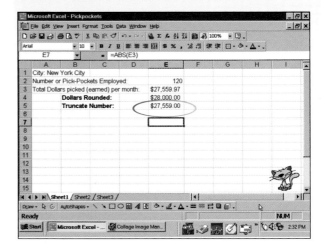

4 Use the INT Function

To use the INT (integer) function, select it from the **Math & Trig** category in the Paste Function dialog box. You use the INT function to display an integer (whole number) value. There are no decimal places to move in the INT function's dialog box; the value is always rounded down to the nearest whole number.

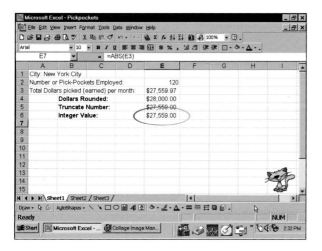

5 Use the ABS Function

The ABS function is used to calculate a number's absolute value; it has nothing to do with abdominal exercises. All ABS really does is make negative numbers positive. Positive numbers are not affected. The ABS function's dialog box has no fields other than one in which you enter the cell address that contains the number you're converting.

	A	B	C	D	E	F
1	City: New York City					
2	Number or Pick-Pockets Employed:				120	
3	Total Dollars picked (earned) per month:				$27,559.97	
4	**Dollars Rounded:**				$28,000.00	
5	**Truncate Number:**				$27,559.00	
6	**Integer Value:**				$27,559.00	
7	**ABS Function:**				27559.97	
8						

End

How-To Hints

Messing with Existing Values

To ROUND, TRUNC, INT, or ABS a value already in a cell, do some editing. Press the **F2** key and then type the formula *around* the value: **=ABS(the value)**. The existing value is edited to appear inside the function. You get your instant result when you press **Enter**.

How to Use the LOOKUP Function

Organize some information into rows and columns, and the LOOKUP function can, well, look up a specific bit of information—a reference, price, part number, description, holding bin, or whatever. Excel offers the traditional LOOKUP function, as well as two more powerful cousins: VLOOKUP, used when the information you're looking for is based on the value of the leftmost column in a table, and HLOOKUP, used when the value you're looking for is in the top row of a table. You'll probably use VLOOKUP more often, which is what's demonstrated in the steps that follow.

Begin

1 Locate the LOOKUP Information Cell

The LOOKUP information cell is the one that displays information that VSLOOKUP finds in the table—not the cell containing the value to be looked up. In this example, I'm looking for an entry in the table that has a certain item number in the hopes that I'll find its description, so I've clicked the **Desc.** cell.

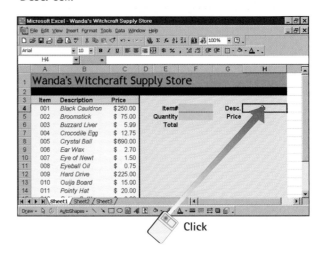

Click

2 Paste the VLOOKUP Function

Open the Paste Function dialog box by clicking on the **Insert** menu and choosing **Function**. Choose the **Lookup & Reference** category and then select the **VLOOKUP** function. Click **OK** to display the VLOOKUP function dialog box.

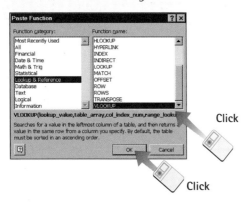

Click

Click

3 Enter the Lookup Value

In the worksheet, click the cell into which you will enter the lookup value. In this case, I've selected the **Item#** cell (**F4**) because I want Excel to look up the description for the product whose item number I enter.

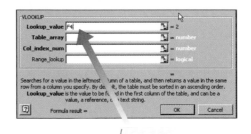

4 Enter the Table Array

In the **Table_Array** field, tell VSLOOKUP where the table is. Simply use your mouse to drag over the table in your worksheet; otherwise, type the table coordinates. In this case, the table starts at A4 and goes through C17, so I've typed **A4:C17**.

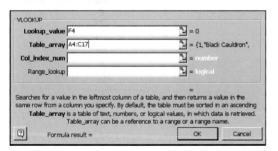

5 Enter the Number of the Column

Enter the number of the column that contains the information you want displayed. For example, if the item price is in the third column, type **3** in the **Col_index_num** field. (Column numbers start with 1.) In this example, I want the description of the product; descriptions are listed in column 2, so I've entered **2**. Leave the Range_Lookup field blank. Click **OK**.

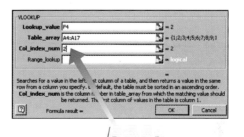

6 Type an Item Number

The formula is inserted into your worksheet. Type a lookup value (in this example, an item number), and watch as the lookup information (in this case, a description) pops up.

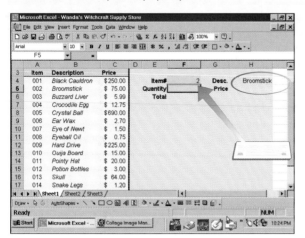

End

How-To Hints

And the #N/A Means What?

The #N/A warning appears in cells that cannot, for some reason, display a value. For the LOOKUP functions, it probably means you haven't specified a value to look up.

It Displays Random Values

There's an overlooked warning in the Paste Function dialog box about the VLOOKUP function: The items in the table's far-left column must be sorted in ascending order. If they aren't, the VLOOKUP function will not return the proper values.

All About the Range_Lookup Value

The final item in the VLOOKUP function's dialog box is Range_Lookup. That's a true or false option that tells Excel to search for the first, closest match to the lookup value in case the exact value isn't found. A value of 1 or TRUE activates this feature; 0 or FALSE turns it off.

How to Work with Dates

A date is a peculiar thing in a spreadsheet. Not like a blind date or even (gasp!) a computer date, Excel stores dates and even time values as numbers inside a cell. The difference is how the number is displayed; cells containing dates are displayed in a date *format*.

Of course, the idea here is that by having dates stored as numbers you can do things with them. You can, for example, subtract two dates to find out how old something is, create a list of dates each three days apart, or just chuck all the math and type in a date as you'd type in a value.

Begin

1 Enter Your Birth Date

The easiest way to type a date into a worksheet is as a date. For example, if you type **10/19/1960** (be sure to type out the full year), it will be interpreted by Excel as October 19, 1960. Note: If you type **October 19**, it'll be interpreted as October 19 of the current year—and it might be displayed as 19-Oct. (For more information of formatting dates, refer to Chapter 5.)

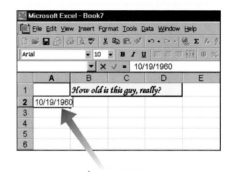

2 Paste the TODAY() Function

Move down one cell and type **=TODAY()**. This pastes in the TODAY function, which returns today's date.

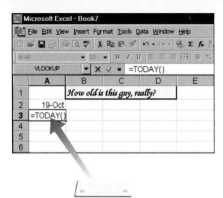

3 Subtract the Two Cells

In a third cell, subtract your birthday from today's date by typing the addresses of the cells that hold this information. I've typed **=A3[ms]A2** in this example because today's date is listed in cell A3, and my birthday is listed in cell A2.

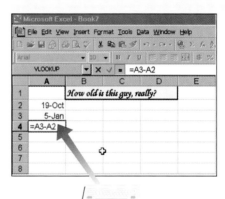

4 Press Ctrl+1

Press **Enter** and you see...a date! You'll need to reformat the cell as a general value to see how many days old you are. (Formatting is covered in a future chapter, so this is a sneak peek.) With the new date cell selected, press **Ctrl+1**. This displays the Format Cells dialog box. Choose **General** from the **Category** list and then click **OK**.

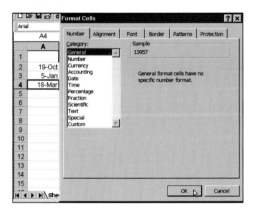

5 Calculate Your Age in Years

The value displayed in the worksheet tells you how many days old you are, which may or may not be particularly useful. To find out how many years old you are, divide the difference between the two cells by 365. You need to use parentheses to get the proper result; in this example, I've typed **(A3-A2)/365**. You need to press **Ctrl+1** to reformat the value as a general value instead of a date.

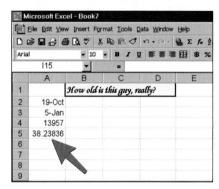

End

How-To Hints

Drag-Filling Dates

Instead of entering a simple series of dates by hand, you can drag to create a series of dates; start with a date in one cell, then drag the mouse to select a row or column of cells. When you drag-fill a date, Excel normally increments the dates by 1. You can use standard Excel formulas to have the date increase by any increment you prefer. For example, if the start date is typed in cell A1, type **=A1+7** in cell A2 to have the series increase by a week for each row. Drag cell A2 down to create your series.

What Are the Values, Really?

Excel keeps track of the date as a number. For example, January 1, 1999, is day number 36,161. January 2 iss 36,162. The information is displayed by Excel as a date, but because each day has a number, you can do math with dates. (The "first day" according to Excel, was January 1, 1900.) If the date value contains a decimal part, as in 36162.9191, then the decimal part represents a *time* value. For example, .9191 is just about 10:00 p.m.; .5 would be noon.

Displaying the Date Value

You can display the value for a date by typing the date and reformatting the cell with **Ctrl+1**. If it's just the number you're after, use the DATE function, which returns the value for any date you enter. For example, **DATE(1993,2,3)** returns the date value for February 3, 1993.

Task

5

Making Your Data Presentable

*D*ata is not pronounced *dat-uh*. It's pronounced *DAY-tuh*. Okay, we're picking nits here, but in a computer, data means information. It's important. It's the data or information that the computer consumes, and data that is produced. Good data means good information. Good data in means good data out.

In a worksheet, data is the information—text, values, and formulas—that you type into various cells. The data is massaged by Excel to produce some sort of desired result. That's the idea. But how does it look? Data by itself is boring. Sure, raw data may be informative, but it's not *inspiring*. And that's sad; given all the powerful formatting tools Excel has, there's just no excuse for producing a meaningless grid full of weary 10-point Arial text and numbers. You want to hand over a report and wow them.

Formatting makes your worksheet (and eventually printed information) pretty and gives it zip. Yes, it's the information that's important, but why not spice things up with some fonts or big text? Cut loose! Be wild! Drive the point home with some borders, shading, and even color.

Excel lets you do amazing things with the information you stuff into a cell. It's a virtual carnival of formatting mirth, a place in which to frolic and dawdle. Go ahead and make your data charming and presentable. ●

How to Format Numbers

Formatting numbers is a small part of the big picture, which is formatting cells. In Excel, you handle cell formatting by selecting the **Cells** command in the **Format** menu; this displays the handy Format Cells dialog box. While there are lots of toys and goodies inside that dialog box for formatting a cell any which way, the bulk of the dialog box is geared toward formatting plain old numbers—which need not be plain nor old, providing that you use the box properly.

Begin

1 Open the Format Cells Dialog Box

Excel lets you be plain and boring when you want to. It's called the General format. To apply it, choose the cell (or cells) you want to format and the **Format** menu, then **Cells**. In the Format Cells dialog box, click the **Number** tab.

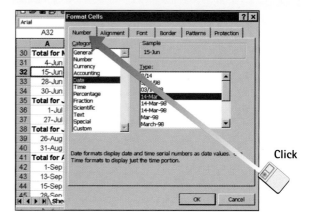

Click

2 Choose General

Click **General** in the **Category** list. Notice that the Sample area shows a preview of how the selected value will be displayed. Click **OK** to apply that (boring) format to the selected cell.

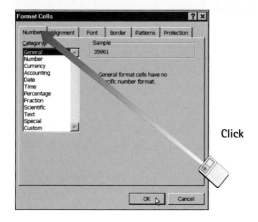

Click

3 Format a Cell with a Decimal

To format a cell that has a decimal part, select the cell and choose **Cells** from the **Format** menu. In the Number tab, choose **Number** from the **Category** list. Choose various options to control how the value is displayed and then click **OK**.

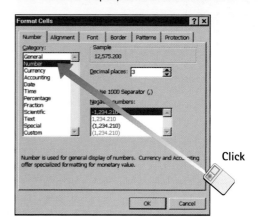

Click

4 Line Up Decimal Places

Sometimes you have a column of single-digit numbers and other numbers with decimal values. To make things look better, select all the values in the column and open **Format Cells**. Choose **Number** from the **Number** tab. Enter **1** (or whatever value you want) in the **Decimal Places** field to give all the numbers one decimal place. Click **OK**.

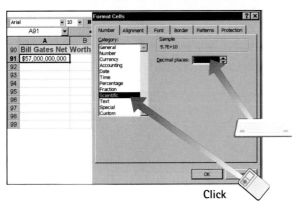

Before

After

5 Display a Fraction

Excel can magically figure out that .5 is 1/2 or that .333 is 1/3. All you need to do is format the value as a fraction. Simply select the cell containing the value you want to change and open the Format Cells dialog box. Choose **Fraction** from the category list in the **Number** tab and then select the type of fraction you want. Click **OK**.

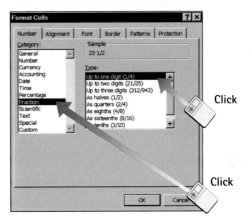

Click

Click

6 Display Scientific Notation

Scientific notation is used for numbers so vast that you have to be a scientist to understand or use them. Seriously, scientific (or *E*) notation is used to express large values that would otherwise look dorky in a cell—like Bill Gates's net worth. To use that format, select the cell and open the Format Cells dialog box, click the **Number** tab, choose **Scientific**, and enter a number in the Decimal Places box.

Click

End

How-To Hints

How to Enter a Fraction

Excel's shortcut for entering a fraction into a cell is to type the value, a space, and then the fraction. So 14 1/2 is calculated by Excel to the value 14.5, but it's displayed as **14 1/2**. Use 0 to enter the fraction part only—as in 0 3/4—to display 3/4 (or .75).

Special Formats

The Special category in the Number tab of the Format Cells dialog box allows you to format four unusual numbers: zip codes, phone numbers, and social security numbers. These aren't traditional values (in that you probably won't do math with them), but Excel has formats available even so. The final category in the Number tab of the Format Cells dialog box—the Custom category—lets you create your own formats using special symbols and codes only an advanced Excel user would appreciate.

How to Format Dollars and Cents

Excel isn't an accounting package. Still, to be honest, a lot of monetary things go on in a worksheet. It can be avoided, of course; our view of Excel is that it's a program that manipulates any type of information that can fit into a grid. But, hey! Money fits into a grid. A general ledger is a grid. And after all, spreadsheets have their root in accounting. Like it or not, the most common thing you'll be formatting in Excel will probably be dollars and cents. The money stuff. Bottom line. Greed.

Begin

1 Select the Cell(s)

Select the cell or group of cells you want to format as dollars and cents—or any other monetary value.

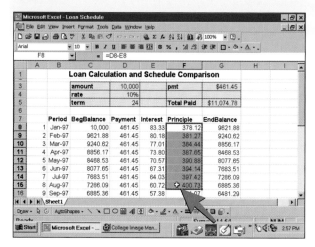

2 Open the Format Cells Dialog Box

Choose **Cells** from the **Format** menu. The Format Cells dialog box appears. In the Numbers tab, select one of two categories for formatting monetary values: **Currency** or **Accounting**. Accounting is identical to Currency, but without the capacity to handle negative numbers, so this task covers Currency only.

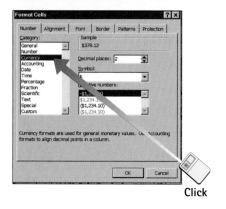

Click

3 Adjust the Settings

The standard Currency setting is two decimal places and a dollar sign, and negative numbers shown in parentheses (a standard accounting practice) and in red. You can mess around if you like. For example, choose the new Euro symbol if you want to display Euro amounts in your worksheet (a new fad). Alternatively, leave it on dollars and click **OK**.

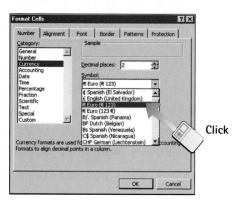

Click

4 View the Results

The cells you selected in step 1 are formatted in dollars and cents.

End

How-To Hints

The $ Shortcut

Any time you want to enter a monetary value, start it with the dollar sign. That displays the dollar sign in the cell and tells Excel to format the value as dollars and cents. You can use the Format Cells dialog box to make further formatting adjustments, if necessary.

The $ Button on the Toolbar

Another way to quickly format (or reformat) a cell or selected group of cells is to click the **Currency Style** button (the one with the dollar sign) on the toolbar.

What? No Decimal Places?

If you choose to display dollar amounts without decimal places, don't fret over losing your common cents; Excel still keeps track of the "real" value in the cell. Only the displayed value is shown without the decimal part.

The $'s Position

If you notice that the currency symbol is sometimes next to a value and other times it's off to the left, blame the Accounting category format. To change this, reformat the cell in the **Currency** format. (The Accounting format lines up the currency symbol and decimal point for a column of cells.)

How to Format Percentages

A percentage is another common way to express values in a spreadsheet. We're big percentage fans, preferring them in many cases over unchanging values. For example, you could have a budget dictating that you put 5 percent of your earnings away in savings every month, but since you earn $2,000 you know it will always be $100. Even so, you're still better off entering a percentage; should your income change, the savings amount changes along with it. Very clever, these percentage people.

Begin

1 Choose the Cells to Format

Select the cell(s) that contain a value or formula whose result you want expressed as a percent. Note that percentages are typically values below 1, which itself is 100 percent; values greater than 1 are greater than 100 percent. This isn't bad, we're just mentioning it here since some folks may enter 57 instead of .57 and get 5700%!

2 Choose the Percentage Category

Choose **Format** from the menu and then choose **Cells** to open the Format Cells dialog tab. Choose **Percentage** in the Number tab's Category list and then decide how many decimal places should be displayed with the percent. Click **OK**.

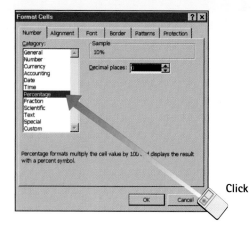

Click

3 View the Results

The cell's new format displays the value as a percentage.

4 The Percentage Shortcut

To enter any value as a percentage in Excel without going through the rigamarole of opening the Format Cells dialog box, just type the number and tack a percent sign on the end. For instance, typing **57%** puts the value .57 in a cell and displays it as **57%**.

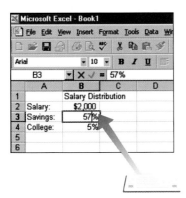

End

How-To Hints

What Is a Percentage?

A percent is literally how many items per 100 there are. (*Cent* is Latin for 100). 50 out of 100 is 50%. For values other than 100, you can use the is-over-of formula: **is/of**. For example, what percentage *is* 47 *of* 138? Take the *is* value, 47, and divide it by the *of* value, 138. You get .34 (plus change), which Excel can format as a percent value.

Adjusting the Decimals

You can change the number of decimal places displayed in a percent by using the **Increase Decimal** or **Decrease Decimal** buttons on the toolbar. If you decrease the decimals, Excel rounds the decimal value up or down accordingly.

How to Format Dates and Times

Goldilocks was a trespasser and thief, but her story teaches us a valuable lesson: Some things are too extreme one way, and others are too extreme another way, but there's always that one thing that's *just right*. You'll discover this as you work with dates in Excel. To prove this, type a date as January 27; Excel displays it as 27-Jan. Type 1-99, and you get Jan-99. Type 1/27/99 and you get 1/27/99. Why go mad? Just type the date or time any old way and then use the Format Cells dialog box to format it the way you want, which is *just right*.

Begin

1 Select a Cell with a Date

Select a cell(s) that has a date value entered (or enter a date yourself). Dates can be entered as month and day; month and year; or day, month, and year. (You should use hyphens instead of slashes to enter dates; although Excel accepts the slash character, it may interpret 1/99 as "one divided by 99".)

	A	B	C	D
		Important Family Dates		
4	Birthdates		Wedding Anniversary	
6	Jeremiah Gookin	6/1/95		
7	Jonah Gookin	1/20/94		
8	Simon Gookin	2/4/93		
9	Jordan Gookin	18-Mar-87		
10	Shirley Hardin	4/6/36	4/16/55	
11	Virgil Hardin	October 21, 1935	4/16/55	
12	Debra Coppernoll	2/14/56	1/31/56	

B6 = 6/1/1995

2 Choose the Date Category

Open the Format Cells dialog box by opening the **Format** menu, then choosing **Cells**. Choose **Date** from the Category list in the Number tab. The dialog box displays several formats for displaying the date. Select one you like, and click **OK**.

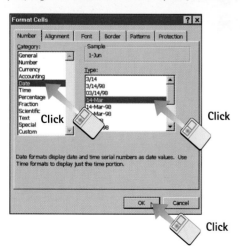

Click

Click

Click

3 View the Results

The cell (or group of cells) is formatted as the type of date you specified.

	Important Family Dates	
	Birthdates	Wedding Anniversary
Jeremiah Gookin	1-Jun	
Jonah Gookin	20-Jan	
Simon Gookin	4-Feb	
Jordan Gookin	18-Mar	
Shirley Hardin	6-Apr	16-Apr
Virgil Hardin	21-Oct	16-Apr
Debra Coppernoll	14-Feb	31-Jan

4 Choose a Cell with a Time

To format the way time is displayed, choose a cell containing a time value. This one here is listed in hours:minutes format. Seconds can also be included. Note that Excel assumes AM unless you type in PM or enter the time in 24-hour format.

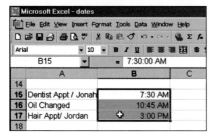

5 Choose the Time Category

Open the Format Cells dialog box by selecting **Cells** from the **Format** menu. Choose **Time** from the Category list in the Number tab. Excel has many time formats to choose from; you might want to choose various items from the Type list to see how they affect how the time value is displayed. When you find a format you like, click **OK**.

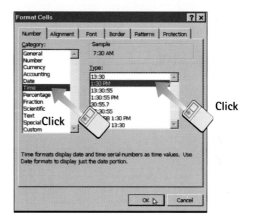

Click

Click

6 View the Results

The cell (or group of cells) containing the time value is re-formatted.

14		
15	Dentist Appt / Jonah	7:30:00
16	Oil Changed	10:45:00
17	Hair Appt/ Jordan	15:00:00
18		

End

How-To Hints

Windows Also Affects the Format

The format used to display the date and time on your computer is actually set in Windows' Control Panel, under Regional Settings.

Random, Related Formulas

Excel also comes with several date and time functions. For example, TODAY() is equal to the current day and time and NOW() returns the date and time right now. See the Date & Time category in the Paste Function dialog box for more information. And that Y2K thing? Excel accepts lots of dates, from January 1, 1900 through December 31, 9999. As long as you enter a four-digit date, Excel accepts those values. If you enter a two-digit date, Excel assumes that 30 through 99 represents the dates 1930 through 1999. Values of 00 through 29 represent the twenty-first century dates 2000 through 2029.

How to Align a Cell

Aligning a cell has nothing to do with politics, though the results are similar. You can align a cell to the left (left justified), right (right justified), or in the middle (centered), and the contents remain the same.

Cell alignment is a visual thing. Excel does a lot of aligning by itself; values are lined up along the right margin and text is lined up along the left margin. You can change this by lining up a cell's contents to whichever way suits the look of your worksheet.

Begin

1 Select Cells to Align

Select a cell or group of cells whose contents you want to align. By default, values are right aligned, while text left aligned.

2 Center the Cells' Contents

The formatting toolbar has three alignment buttons: Align Left, Center, and Align Right. To center the contents of the selected cells, click the **Center** button.

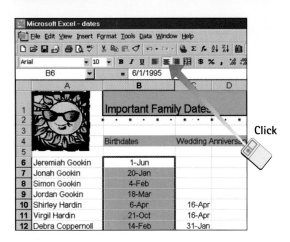

Click

3 Left Align the Cells' Contents

Click the **Align Left** button to slam the contents of your cells over to the cells' left edge.

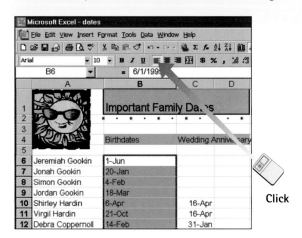

Click

4 Unalign the Cells

To unalign a cell, you must remove that cell's formatting. Choose the cells you want to unalign, then open the **Edit** menu and choose **Clear Formats**. This removes the cell's formatting but leaves the value intact.

	Important Family Dates	
	Birthdates	Wedding Anniversary
Jeremiah Gookin	1-Jun	
Jonah Gookin	20-Jan	
Simon Gookin	4-Feb	
Jordan Gookin	18-Mar	
Shirley Hardin	6-Apr	16-Apr
Virgil Hardin	21-Oct	16-Apr
Debra Coppernoll	14-Feb	31-Jan

End

How-To Hints

Checking Alignment

The alignment buttons on the toolbar can tell you how a cell is aligned. For example, the Right Align button appears selected on the toolbar if you choose a right-aligned cell.

How to Fit Text into a Cell

Though at times it seems that numbers are all that should go into a worksheet's cell, the truth is that all cells are designed to hold either numbers or text. Of course, it seems awfully unfair to try to jam text into a teensy tiny cell, doesn't it? Cells are too confining. Words want to be free! They yearn for the expanse of a word processor's endless sheet of paper. To make your words feel better inside a cramped cell, Excel offers you a whole slab of juicy text-formatting options. Prepare to have fun with them all.

Begin

1 Open the Alignment Tab

Once you've selected a cell or group of cells that you want to format, open the Format Cells dialog box by choosing **Format, Cells**. Click the **Alignment** tab to see your text alignment options.

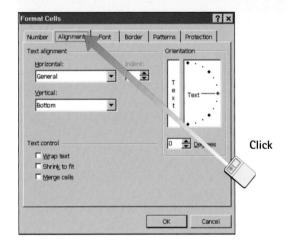

Click

2 Choose a Horizontal Alignment

The **Horizontal** drop-down list aligns text left to right, similarly to the alignment buttons on the toolbar (see Task 5). Additionally, you can use the Fill or Justify options to align text in cells.

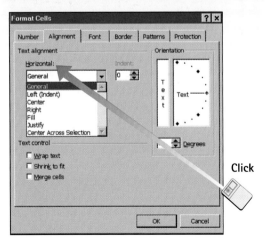

Click

3 Choose a Vertical Alignment

The **Vertical** drop-down list contains options for aligning text in an up-and-down manner: Top aligns text to the top of the cell; Bottom aligns text to the bottom; Center aligns text to the center; Justify inserts space between multiple lines to fill the cell's height with text.

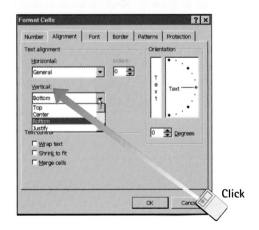

Click

4 Choose a Fancy Orientation

If your neck is out of alignment, you can adjust the text in Excel to appear at almost any angle using the Orientation area of the Format Cells dialog box's Alignment tab. Either use your mouse to select an angle or manually enter an angle (in degrees) in the Degrees spin box. Alternatively, click the tall, skinny window to display your text vertically.

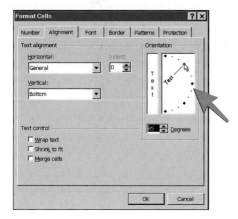

5 Set Text Control Options

Choose the **Wrap Text** option if you want the text to stay inside the cell. Excel will normally extend text over the next few cells (to the right or left, depending on the alignment). Use the **String to Fit** option to make your text as small as possible (size-wise) so that it all fits in the cell. When you're satisfied with your choices, click **OK**.

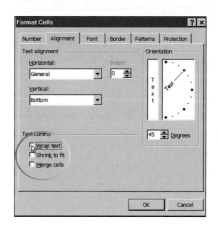

6 View the Results

The alignment formatting you selected is applied to your cells when you click the **OK** button.

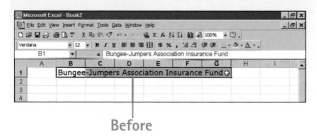

Before

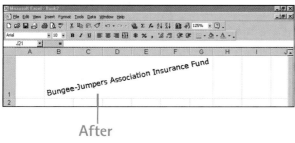

After

How-To Hints

Changing the Format of the Cell

Changing the text alignment in a cell is only one option. Another option might be to change the cell's size. See Chapter 6, "Sprucing Up the Worksheet," for more information.

Save Complex Formats as Styles

If you create a text format you like, you can save it as a style in Excel. That way, the format can be reapplied quickly to other cells. See Chapter 6 for more information on creating styles.

End

How to Change Your Text

In the beginning, you created a worksheet. And the worksheet was empty and visually boring. Even when you added text, you beheld it in a dull and empty style. And there was woe among the cells.

Unless you tell Excel otherwise, it uses the Arial font at 10 points to display information in your worksheet. I need not rant on how absolutely uninspiring that is, especially given all the fonts and sizes and text attributes—and color—you can use to mix up a batch of interesting text. Be bold. Or at least be italic.

Begin

1 Choose a Cell to Format

Select a cell you want to format. The cell can be empty, but it's always better to have text or a value in the cell you choose so you get visual feedback. You can choose one cell, a group of cells, or the entire worksheet. (Press **Ctrl+A** to select the whole worksheet.)

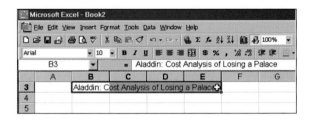

2 Open the Font Tab

Open the Format Cells dialog box by either opening the **Format** menu and choosing Cells or pressing **Ctrl+1**. Click the **Font** tab to display font-formatting information.

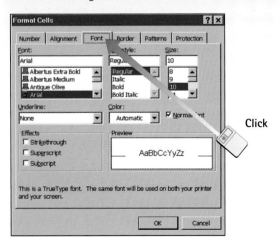

Click

3 Choose a Font (Typestyle)

Fonts are listed alphabetically in the Font list box. Select a font and then see how it looks by checking out the Preview part of the tab.

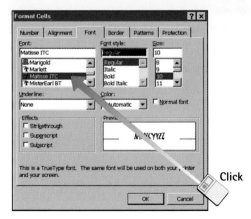

Click

4 Choose a Font Style

Select a style from the Font Style list. The styles in this list include basic text effects: regular, **bold**, *italic*, or **bold italic**. To underline your text, select an underline style from the Underline drop-down list. To apply other text effects, check any of the boxes in the Effects area.

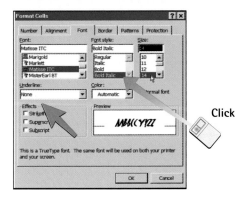

Click

5 Choose a Font Size

Select a font size from the Size list. The size values are measured in points (there are 72 points to an inch). Ten points is the boring size Excel naturally uses, but 12 points is much more readable on a printout. Once you've made your selections, click **OK**.

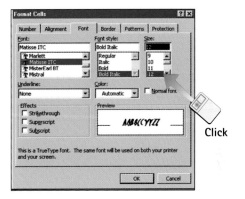

Click

6 View the Results

The font, style, and size you selected are applied to the cell(s) in your document.

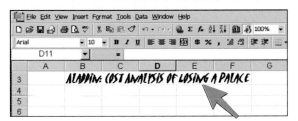

End

How-To Hints

Fonts Are a Windows Thing

Excel uses the same fonts the rest of Windows uses. When you add new fonts to Windows, you add them to Excel.

Changing Only Part of Your Text

Usually, any changes you make in the Font tab of the Format Cells dialog box affect all text in the cell. If you edit the cell (press **F2**) and select part of the text, then the changes made in the Font tab affect only the text you've selected.

Fixing Fonts from the Toolbar

You can also select a font from the drop-down list at the far right of the Formatting toolbar. In addition, you can use the Size drop-down list to the right of the Font drop-down list to adjust the size of your text. To the right of the Size list, you'll find buttons for the bold, italic, and underline text styles. Choosing a cell and clicking any of these buttons displays text in that style.

How to Add Borders

If you want to attract attention, buy yourself a nice hat. If your head is just too big, or if you have very nice hair, ladies might consider some attractive jewelry; the guys, a bright tie. Such fashion statements can shift focus to where you want it.

To attract attention or shift focus in your worksheet, you can use a few nifty formatting tricks. One is to add a border to a cell or group of cells. A fat, dashed, or colored line around all or part of a cell works very nicely for added pizzazz. Patterns or shades can eliminate the "prison of cells" effect too many worksheets have.

Begin

1 Add a Border to a Single Cell

Select a cell, open the **Format** menu, and choose **Cells**. In the Format Cells dialog box, click the **Border** tab. Use the options in the Border tab to choose where you want the border (around all or part of the cell), choose a line style, and, optionally, a color. Click **OK** to apply the border.

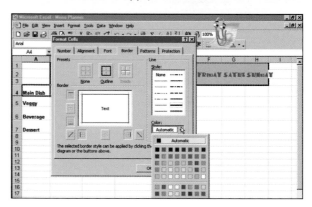

2 Add a Border to a Column

Select a column of cells and then choose **Cells** from the **Format** menu. In the Format Cells dialog box, click the **Border** tab. The preview shown in the Border area reflects the column's cells. Use the tools in the dialog box to set the border, then click **OK**.

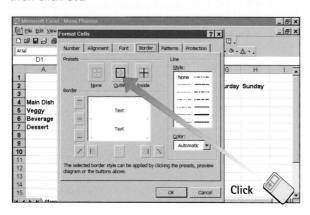

3 Add a Border to a Row

Select a row of cells and then choose **Cells** from the **Format** menu. In the Format Cells dialog box, click the **Border** tab. Optionally, set the line style and color and then experiment with the border options until you find one you like. Click **OK**.

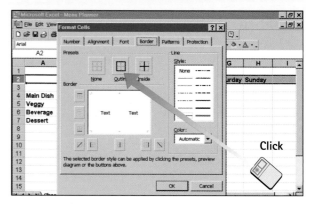

4 Add Borders to a Block

Select a block of cells and then choose **Cells** from the **Format** menu. In the Format Cells dialog box, click the **Border** tab. Choose various options for setting the border line style, color, and position, and click **OK** to apply the border.

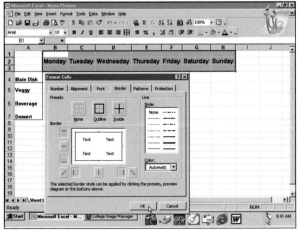

End

How-To Hints

Not Getting the Right Lines?

You must choose the line style before you click in the Border area of the dialog box to set a cell border. The same goes for color: Pick a color value and then set the lines you want in that color.

Using the Border Button

The Border button on the toolbar can be used to instantly apply a border to any cell or selected group of cells. Click the **down arrow** by the Border button to see a menu of various border options. (Line style and color can be set only in the Border tab of the Format Cells dialog box.)

Quickly Removing Borders

The easiest way to quickly remove a cell's border is to use the **Border** button on the toolbar. Choose the "empty" cell pattern from the drop-down list to remove all borders from your cell or from a group of selected cells.

How to Add Patterns and Color

If you've ever approached a wall with a bucket of paint and a brush and had second thoughts, don't worry. Excel lets you color lots of things, including patterns, borders, text, and the cell's background. Proper use of colors and patterns can greatly improve your worksheet's presentation and readability. Of course, you need a color printer for color output—either that, or use crayons to color black-and-white output.

Begin

1 Open the Patterns Tab

Select a group of empty cells to which you want to apply a pattern. Open the **Format** menu and choose **Cells**. Click the **Patterns** tab in the Format Cells dialog box; click the **Pattern** button to view a pop-up list of patterns and colors for those patterns.

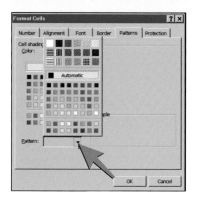

2 Choose a Pattern

Select a pattern from the pop-up list; the pattern will appear in the preview part of the dialog box. Optionally, you can click the **Pattern** button again and select a color for your pattern. Click **OK**; the cells in your worksheet are coated with the selected pattern.

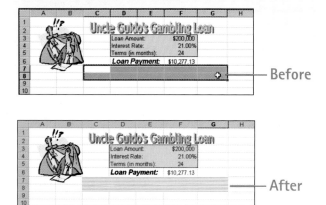

Before

After

3 Change the Text Color

Choose the cell(s) in which you want to change the text color. Open the **Format** menu, choose **Cells**, and click the **Font** tab in the **Format Cells** menu. Click the **Color** drop-down list to display the color palette and choose a color for your text. You'll see a preview in the Preview area; click **OK**.

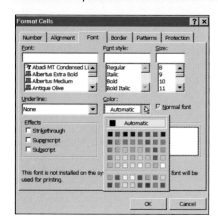

4 View the Results

The color you've selected is applied to text in the selected cell(s). Whatever color you chose is applied to any information displayed in the cell, including text, values, or the result of some formula.

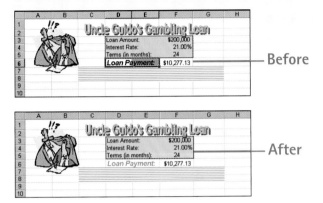
Before

After

5 Set a Background Color

Choose the cell or group of cells whose background you want to fill. Open the **Format** menu, choose **Cells**, and click the **Patterns** tab. Finally, select any color in the Color area as a background color. The default white background and gridlines between cells are overwritten by the color you choose.

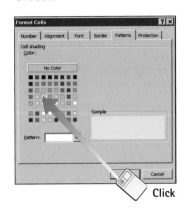
Click

6 View the Results

The color is applied to the cell(s).

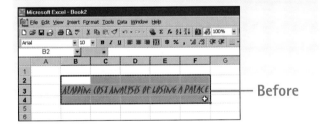
Before

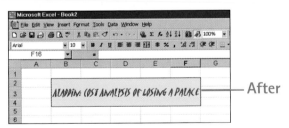
After

End

How-To Hints

Use the Font Color Button

The **Font Color** button (the one with a capital A on top of a color bar) on the Formatting toolbar can be used to instantly apply color to your text. Click the button to apply the color shown under the A. Alternatively, click the **down-arrow button** next to the A to display a color palette and choose from there.

Use the Fill Color Button

You can use the **Fill Color** button (the one that has a paint can that looks like it's about to tip over) on the Formatting toolbar to apply a background color to any cell or selected group of cells. The button itself displays the current fill color (below the paint bucket). Clicking the button applies that color. Alternatively, you can click the **down-arrow button** next to the bucket and choose another color from the color menu.

How to Undo Formatting

"Mommy, I made you a painting," he says so innocently. And he's sincere, too. He's made it just for you, probably using materials he's found around the house: chalk, butter, your lipstick, crayon—what he'll learn in college is a "multimedia" effort. The canvas, of course, is the dining room wall. How thoughtful.

As you approach your worksheet, Format Cells dialog box in hand, it may dawn upon you that you're no better at formatting than a 4-year-old with an odd set of tools. But fear not: You have a handy Undo command at your disposal.

Begin

1 Choose Undo from the Edit Menu

Excel's Undo command removes whatever formatting you just applied. If you goof up, open the **Edit** menu and choose **Undo**.

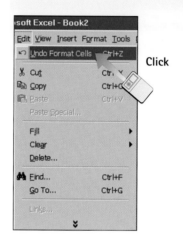

Click

2 Choose Edit, Clear, Formats

If Undo just won't clear up the problem, open the **Edit** menu, choose **Clear**, and select **Formats**. This removes all cell formatting from one cell or from a group of selected cells; it also removes the formatting without changing the cell's contents. (It does remove number formatting in addition to font and color formatting.)

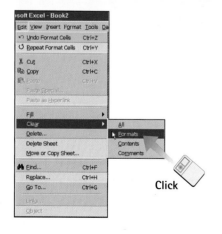

Click

3 Use the Ctrl+Z Keyboard Shortcut

Press **Ctrl+Z** to undo the last step you just did. This could be something you typed, undoing an image you pasted, or undoing something you cut (which would put the object or text you cut back into place).

Ctrl + Z

4 Click the Undo Button

The **Undo** button on the toolbar works just like the **Ctrl+Z** shortcut. It puts the last step back in place.

5 Click the Arrow Key Next to Undo

The Undo button lists the last 10 actions that you can choose undo. Just click the **arrow key** next to the Undo button; the previous 10 items are listed. Caution: The descriptions are not very precise, so you may not have a clue what the item refers to.

End

How-To Hints

Delete Key Won't Work

While pressing the **Delete** key will remove a cell's contents, it does not change the cell's formatting. You'll discover this if you re-type information into a cell and find the format still alive!

Using the Automatic Format

Many formatting commands have an Automatic option, usually for the color. If you want to remove formatting from a cell, choosing the Automatic format often removes the format without otherwise affecting the cell's appearance. For example, choose the **Automatic** color, not black, to restore a cell to black text.

Task

6

Sprucing Up the Worksheet

Genius can be defined as seeing the obvious before anyone else does. It's kind of like a mental race in which the first person to come up with the answer is a genius. That doesn't make the rest of us idiots for thinking of something profound on our own; it just makes us tardy.

Of all the things you could be a genius at, computer knowledge has to be on top the list. For example, someone could claim to be a genius with rocket science. How could you prove him wrong? Anyone gifted enough in the art of verbal baloney could fake being a rocket genius any day of the week, but that doesn't make him a genius.

When it comes to computers, so many of us are often declared geniuses just because we've figured out something before someone else. For some reason it doesn't matter if what we've figured out came out of a book or a manual, just the fact that you can recall it and put it to use makes you the ubiquitous computer genius. Being there first isn't the issue.

So do you want to be a computer genius with Excel?

Honestly, knowing all the formulas or keyboard shortcuts in Excel won't make you look like a genius. Sure, you might be a genius, but that's not important. Looking like a genius is what's important. It's a lot like verbal baloney, but in a visually stunning sense.

While anyone can format and spruce up a worksheet (as the previous chapter shows), it takes a true (between you and me) computer genius to create a visually impressive worksheet. Okay, so it's the computer that does the real calculations. Who cares?! By sprucing up your worksheet, you cross the finish line into geniushood. This chapter shows you the ropes (but you don't have to tell anyone that when you show them your final product). ●

How to Sort Data

We just had an episode at the local community theater where we had to bring in a handful of volunteers to sort out a mailing by zip code. Oh, it was a lot of fun—community spirit, camaraderie, volunteerism, yadda-yadda. The problem: It was unnecessary. The computer itself could have sorted the list for us. Drat! (Too bad we don't have any volunteers well versed in Excel, huh?)

Excel sorts your data quietly, quickly, and without so much as a yodel of complaining. So you can sort you list by zip code, name, value, IQ, or ignorance factor.

Begin

1 Select a Block of Cells

Sorting is kind of a databasey thing, so select a block of cells in your document that contains a table of information, such as names, addresses, or any other type of data that appears in a table.

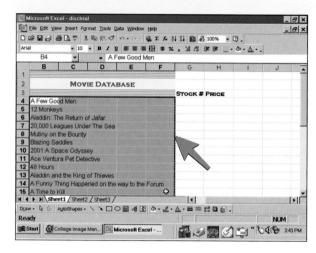

2 Open the Sort Dialog

Open the **Data** menu **and** then choose **Sort** to open the Sort dialog box. This dialog box allows you to sort information in three orders. For example, you can sort by zip code, city, and then last name if you like. (Remember, this all works best if your information is organized in the block cells like a table.)

3 Select Sorting Options

The most common option is to sort information alphabetically. Choose the column you want to sort from the **Sort By** drop-down list and then click on the **Ascending** radio button. If you want to sort subsequent columns, choose them from the **Then By** lists, though this is not required if you're just sorting by one column.

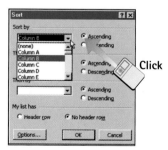

Click

4 Click OK

The information in your worksheet is sorted per your specifications.

	B	C	D	E	F
4	101 Dalmations				
5	12 Monkeys				
6	20,000 Leagues Under The Sea				
7	2001:A Space Odyssey				
8	48 Hours				
9	A Few Good Men				
10	A Funny Thing Happened on the way to the Forum				
11	A Time to Kill				
12	Ace Ventura Pet Detective				
13	Aladdin				
14	Aladdin and the King of Thieves				
15	Aladdin: The Return of Jafar				
16	Blazing Saddles				
17	Mutiny on the Bounty				
18					

End

How-To Hints

Sorting Only One Table Column

You don't have to fill in all Sort By and Then By fields in the Sort dialog box. If you're only sorting your Christmas list by last names, just choose that column and sort away.

Multiple Column Sorts

Sorting with multiple columns allows you to really, really organize a table. When you do this type of sort, it helps to first sort by general information and then by specific information. For example, sort by state, then zip code, then city, then street or last name.

Sort Warning?

Excel may display a Sort Warning dialog box when you select only a single column of cells and choose **Sort** from the **Data** menu. That's because Excel sees data to the right or left of the column you selected and is just trying to be certain you want to sort only that column.

Ahh! The Quick Sort

Two buttons on the standard toolbar let you quickly sort a selected chunk of cells: The Sort Ascending and Sort Descending buttons sort A–Z and Z–A, respectively. The buttons sort based on the leftmost column in the table if you select a table of cells.

How to Change Column Width

Remember that one *Star Trek* episode where they threw Captain Pike into a prison, but the aliens made it very nice? He said that a prison, no matter how nice, was still a prison. How true. And just because the cell in your prison is quite large doesn't mean you're having more fun than the poor schmo in a tiny cell. Information in Excel often feels the same way.

Excel lets you re-size a column, adjusting the width of all the cells in that column. You can make the column as wide as the widest bit of information or adjust the column between very narrow and insufferably wide, all to your heart's content.

Begin

1 Instantly Adjust Column Width

To make a column as wide as the widest piece of information in that column, double-click the line that separates that column's heading from the next column.

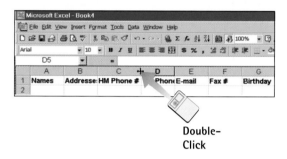

Double-
Click

2 Manually Adjust Column Width

To change the width of a column, point at the line that separates that column's heading from the next column (the mouse pointer changes to a two-arrowed cursor). Drag to the left to shrink the column; drag to the right to expand the column. A ToolTip pops up as you drag, displaying the width of the column in character pitch and pixels.

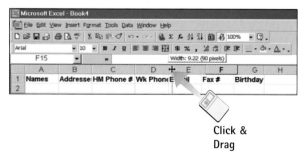

Click &
Drag

3 Select a Group of Columns

Select the column or group of columns you want to re-size by dragging over the column headers (the letters). You can select a single column or group of columns.

4 Open the Column Width Dialog

Open the **Format** menu, choose **Column**, and then select **Width**. The Column Width dialog box appears, allowing you to set either a uniform width for all columns or a specific width for a single column. Values range from 0 to 255 and represent the number of characters that can fit into the cell in a 10-point Arial (boring) font. Entering a value of 0 hides the column.

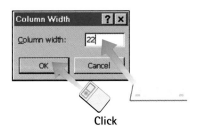

Click

5 Click OK

All the columns you selected now have a uniform width.

End

How-To Hints

Using the AutoFit Command

If you want to adjust a group of columns so that each displays all the information in their cells, open the **Format** menu, choose **Column**, and then click **AutoFit Selection**.

The Old Right-Click Trick

To get quick access to the Column Width dialog box, right-click any column heading and choose **Column Width** from the pop-up menu.

How to Change Row Height

Just as a column of text can be re-sized to fit long values or meandering text, the height of a row can be increased or decreased. Using this trick in conjunction with the column width trick in the previous task, you can actually create perfectly square cells in your worksheet. I have no idea why you would want to do that, but Excel lets you nonetheless.

Begin

1 Instantly Adjust Row Height

To instantly make a row as tall as the tallest bit of information in the row, double-click the line between that row's header and the next row. The row height changes to accommodate the tallest information.

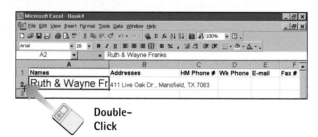

Double-Click

2 Manually Adjust Your Row Height

To change the height of a row by eye-balling it, point at the line that separates that row's heading from the next row and then drag up to decrease the size of the row (or down to increase it). A ToolTip pops up as you drag, displaying the height of the row in character pitch and pixels.

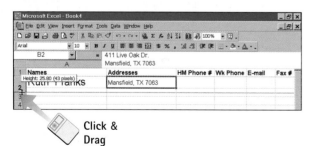

Click & Drag

3 Select a Group of Rows

Either select an entire row by clicking its header or select a group of rows by dragging the mouse over their headers (the row numbers).

4 Open the Row Height Dialog Box

Open the **Format** menu, choose **Row**, and select **Height**. The Row Height dialog box appears, allowing you to set a uniform height for all the rows you've selected. Values entered are in points (the same measurement for the height of a font) and can range from 0 (which hides the row) to 409 (which is a little more than 5 1/2 inches tall).

5 Click OK

All the rows you selected are set to the specified height.

End

How-To Hints

AutoFitting a Row

To set a group of rows so that each row is as tall as the tallest item in it, open the **Format** menu, choose **Row**, and click **Auto Fit**.

Right-Click to Set Row Height

You can reset the height of any row by right-clicking the row's header and choosing **Row Height** from the pop-up menu. This displays the Row Height dialog box, from which you can set the row's height.

TASK 4

How to Check Your Spelling

Excel is not only numbers; it's words. You can fill all the cells with words, phrases, or even poems if you so choose. But where there is text, there is bound to be a spelling error or a typo or two.

Ta-da! It's spell check to the rescue!

Excel's spell checker is a marvelous tool, helping you change *amortise* to *amortize* in a flash. While that's grand, please keep in mind that computer spell checking won't help you catch words that are spelled correctly but used the wrong way, or words that are missing or misused. Still, every little bit helps.

Begin

1 Open the Spelling Dialog Box

Open the **Tools** menu and choose **Spelling** to open the Spelling dialog box. If spelling errors are found, they're displayed in this box, and suggested changes are presented. (If no errors are found, you're told that the spelling check is complete, and you can take a minute to gloat.)

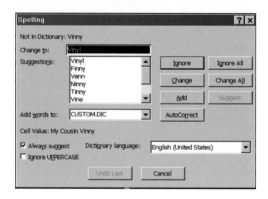

2 Spell the Word Correctly

If the item in the Change To box is correct, click the **Change** button. Otherwise, choose an item from the **Suggestions** list and click **Change**. Click **Ignore** if the word is spelled correctly, but simply unknown to Excel; click **Add** to put the word into Excel's dictionary. (Do this for words you use that are correct but aren't recognized, such as city names, last names, names of other planets and alien races...you know.)

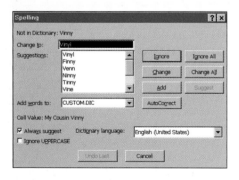

3 Another Misspelled Word...

Excel continues to scan the document for cells containing vile and offensive words until it reaches the end of your document. If you'd like Excel to continue checking at the beginning of the sheet, click **Yes**.

Click

4 Click OK

The spell check is complete.

Click

End

How-To Hints

Take Advantage of AutoCorrect

When the spell checker flags a word you plan on misspelling again (a frequent occurrence), choose the correctly spelled word and click the **AutoCorrect** button in the Spelling dialog box. That way Excel will fix your word as you type it—an amazing thing to behold.

Hey! There's a Toolbar Button

The **Spelling** button on the standard toolbar can be clicked to initiate an immediate documentwide spell check.

The F7 Key

The **F7** key is also a shortcut for starting a spell check—not that a button named F7 serves to remind you of spell checking in any way.

Spell Checking a Few Cells

To spell check only a handful of cells, select them with the mouse. The spell checker then reviews only those cells, without bogging you down by checking the entire worksheet.

I'm Having Trouble with My Novel

Excel is not a word processor. It gives you the luxury of text, but not all the tools necessary to work with text. For writing you need a word processor, such as Microsoft Word, which comes with Excel in the Office 2000 package.

How to Draw Objects

We admit that the title of this task reads like week three in a college art class syllabus—and it very well could be. You know, you just can't title a task in a serious Sams book "Drawing Doodles and Random Nonsense in Your Worksheet." They wouldn't put up with it.

Excel, for some reason, has a complete drawing program embedded in its belly. You can use the drawing program to put circles, squares, lines, and other shapes into your worksheet. Spice it up! Add a cartoon! Express yourself! Go with the flow, but try to appease the art teacher.

Begin

1 Display the Drawing Toolbar

The secret to turning Excel over to a drawing program is to activate the Drawing toolbar. Open the **View** menu, choose **Toolbars**, and then click **Drawing**; alternatively, click the **Drawing** button on the standard toolbar. The Drawing toolbar floats on the bottom of the worksheet (though you can move it around). The tools on that toolbar let you create and manipulate drawings that can float over the worksheet.

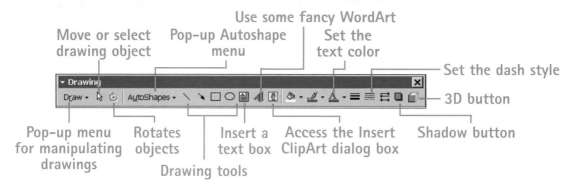

Move or select drawing object

Pop-up Autoshape menu

Use some fancy WordArt

Set the text color

Set the dash style

3D button

Pop-up menu for manipulating drawings

Rotates objects

Insert a text box

Access the Insert ClipArt dialog box

Shadow button

Drawing tools

2 Draw a Line or Arrow

To draw a line, click the **Line** button on the Drawing toolbar and then drag in the worksheet to create the line. To specify a color for the line, select the line, click the **Line Color** button, and select a color from the drop-down list. To set the line style, select the line, click the **Line Style** button, and select a style from the pop-up menu. If you want to draw an arrow, click the **Arrow** button and drag to create the arrow. To choose an arrow style, select the arrow, click the **Arrow Style** button, and select a style from the pop-up menu.

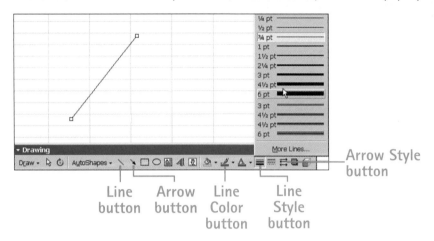

Arrow Style button

Line button   Arrow button   Line Color button   Line Style button

3 Draw a Block or Circle

To draw a block or circle, click the appropriate button on the Drawing toolbar and then drag in the worksheet to create the shape. To create a perfect square or circle, hold down the **Shift** key while dragging. To fill the shape with color, click the **Fill Color** button and select a color from the drop-down list; click in the shape to fill it with the color you selected. Handles on a selected object can be manipulated individually to change the image.

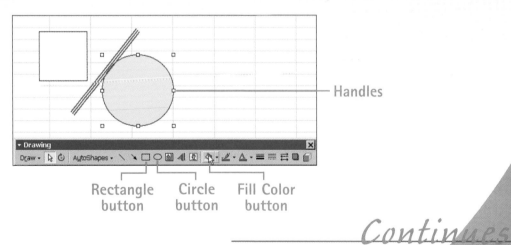

Handles

Rectangle button   Circle button   Fill Color button

Continues

4 Apply a Shadow

To apply shadowing to a block or circle, select the shape you want to shadow, click the **Shadow** button on the toolbar, and then select a shadow type from the pop-up menu.

Shadow is added

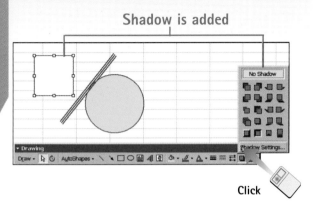

Click

5 Use 3D Styling

To make a block or circle appear 3D, select the shape and then click the **3D button**. Choose the 3D style you want from the pop-up menu.

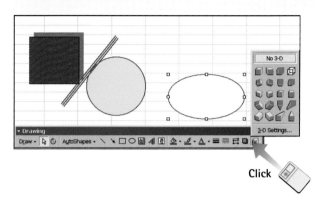

Click

6 Add an AutoShape

Clicking the **AutoShapes** button brings up a menu of items, each of which displays a palette of predefined shapes. For example, choosing Stars and Banners displays various star shapes and banners in which you can write text. Drag in the worksheet to create the AutoShape image; add color to the shape just as you would for a circle or block.

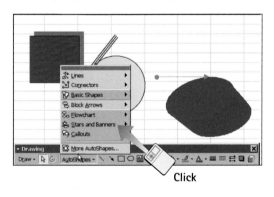

Click

7 Arrange Images

To have one image appear in front of or behind another, select the image you want to rearrange and then click the **Draw** button on the Drawing toolbar. Choose **Order** from the pop-up menu, and then decide how you want to rearrange the selected object.

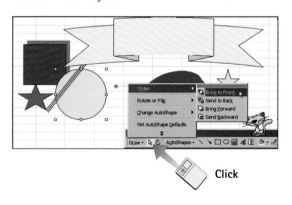

Click

8 Create a Text Box

Click the **Text Box** item on the Drawing toolbar and then drag the mouse in the worksheet to create a text box. A cursor appears inside the box, allowing you to enter text (click elsewhere in the worksheet when you're done typing). Either use the text box's handles to resize it or drag the text box around the sheet using the pointer button. To edit any of the text, right-click in the text box and choose **Edit Text** from the menu.

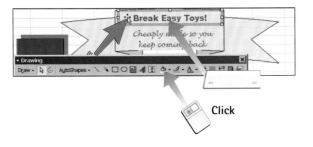

Click

9 Splash in Some WordArt

WordArt enables you to spice up a weary worksheet with some amazing text. Clicking the **WordArt** button displays the WordArt Gallery dialog box. Choose a style from the list and click **OK**. In the Edit WorkArt Text dialog box, type the text you want to appear as WordArt in your document. Select a font and font size, and decide whether you want the text to be bold or italic. The text shows up in the style you chose in the previous step.

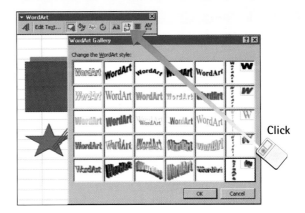

Click

10 Click OK

The WordArt object appears in your worksheet. Like other objects, you can move or re-size it using the Select Object pointer. To edit the text in a WordArt object, double-click the object. When you're done playing Picasso, close the drawing toolbar; open the **View** menu, choose **Toolbars**, and click **Drawing** from the menu (or right-click the Drawing toolbar and choose **Drawing** from the pop-up menu).

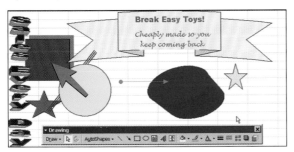

End

How-To Hints

Deleting an Object

To remove an object from the worksheet, click it once to select it and then press the **Delete** key. You can also use the Select Object pointer to drag over several objects and select them as a group. Pressing the **Delete** key removes the bunch.

I Can't Select Any Cells!

The Select Object pointer can be used only to work with graphics and objects in a worksheet. To return to "normal" Excel, click the **Select Object** button on the Drawing toolbar. That restores the mouse to regular operation.

How to Insert ClipArt

Fun, interesting, and useful artwork can be added to your worksheet to give it a lot of oomph—a picture of a jet on an itinerary, a baby bottle on a babysitter's schedule, a stack of cash on a business proposal. You get the idea. Excel has a smattering of ClipArt—freebie images that can, if used right, bring shine to a dull and boring worksheet. Combine ClipArt with colors, fonts, borders, and the whole lot, and people will really be fooled into thinking you know your stuff.

Begin

1 Open the ClipArt Dialog Box

Scroll your worksheet to the spot where you want to splash down some ClipArt. (Unlike other things in Excel, ClipArt hovers over cells in your worksheet, so no cell need be selected.) When you've found your spot, open the **Insert** menu, select **Picture**, and choose **Clip Art**.

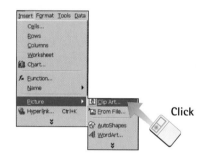
Click

2 Choose a Category

The Insert ClipArt dialog box appears, which contains categories of ClipArt (in addition to being able to add pictures, you can insert sounds—such as the cha-ching sound of a cash register—and motion clips to a worksheet, not to mention borders, buttons, icons, and Web graphics). Click on the **Picture** tab and then scroll through the dialog box until you find a category you think you can use. When you find a category you want, click it.

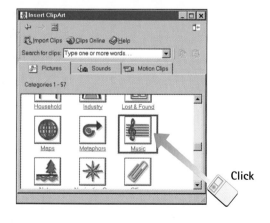
Click

3 Find an Image

Use the **Back** and **Forward** buttons at the top of the dialog box to look at the images in the category you selected in step 2. When you find an image you like, click it to open a pop-up menu. The menu enables you to do various things, such as insert or preview the clip, add the clip to your favorites or some other category, and find a similar clip.

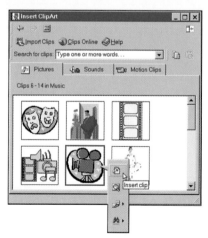

4 Insert the Picture

Click the **Insert Clip** button in the pop-up menu to put the image into your worksheet. Click the **X** button in the upper-right corner of the Insert ClipArt dialog box to remove it from view.

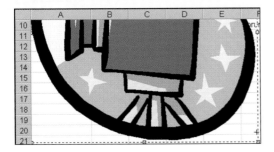

5 Adjust Your Picture

Wow. That's a big picture! Too big, as a matter of fact. On the four corners and sides of the picture are eight boxes, or *adjustment handles*. Your mouse changes to an arrow when it's directly over a box. Go to the corner handle and drag the handle inward (toward the center of the picture) to re-size the picture to something more reasonable. You may also need to adjust the column width and row height to make things look right. (This may be a good time to mention that more isn't always better when it comes to ClipArt; sometimes it's just more.)

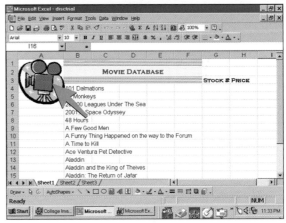

End

How-To Hints

Deleting ClipArt

If your picture doesn't look right and you want to get rid of it, just click it and press the **Delete** key. Bye-bye.

Buy More Art

The ClipArt section of Excel is limited. If you want to use additional art from one of those 25,000 super cool ClipArt CDs, from the Web, or from your hard drive, you can do that, too. Open the **Insert** menu, choose **Picture**, and select **From File** to open an image file stored on your hard drive. (Save the image from the Web or the CD there first.)

More Art Adjustments

For more cropping options, adjusting its size and the like, right-click on your art and choose **Format Picture**. Go ahead and play a bit!

How to Change the Worksheet's Background

Why bore yourself typing numbers into a grid on a white background? With Excel, you can have any image on your hard drive as the worksheet's background.

Begin

1 Open the Sheet Background Dialog

Open the Sheet Background Dialog by clicking the **Format** menu, choosing **Sheet**, and selecting **Background**.

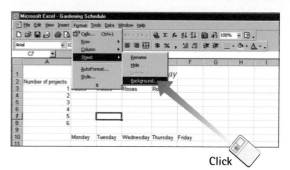

Click

2 Find a Graphics File

Excel can read just about any graphics file format; use the **Sheet Background** dialog box like an **Open** dialog box to find a graphics file for your worksheet's background (see the How-To Hints for information on finding images). Click a file to view a preview in the **Sheet Background** dialog's right-hand pane. To insert the graphic, click the **Insert** button.

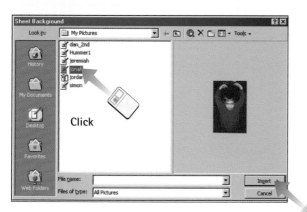

Click

Click

3 View the Results

Your worksheet has a pretty background image, which is tiled to fill the entire worksheet.

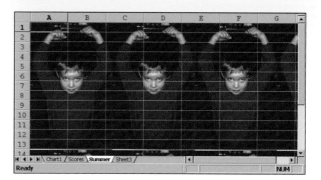

4 Remove the Background

To remove the background image, open the **Format** menu, choose **Sheet**, and select **Delete Background**. The background image is gone and boring white returns.

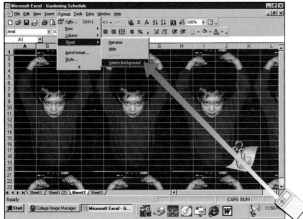

Click

End

How-To Hints

Getting Background Pictures

There are some images in the Windows folder on your hard drive, but otherwise you'll need to generate your own images for use as backgrounds, either by using a graphics program or scanner, or by copying files from the Web.

Choosing Images

The best background pictures are soft, light images, like clouds or soft, distant images. The sample background shown here is cute, but you wouldn't be able see any of the typing.

How to Create Styles

It's addicting to get fancy and play with formatting your cells. That fun can turn to tedium when you have to format a whole chorus line of cells identically; what was once engrossing becomes a pain.

Why should it? After all, isn't the computer supposed to enjoy doing repetitive things for you? Welcome to the Style command. A *style* is, in a nutshell, a collection of formats that are applied to a single cell. This enables you to stick text or numbers in a cell and have it immediately formatted by the style.

This task is the first step in using styles, creating a style out of various formatting commands you've used in your worksheet. This part requires you to be creative and fancy, using all that goo that makes the creative side of your brain work. (Task 9 covers style application.)

Begin

1 Open the Style Dialog Box

Use the various commands to format a cell. Change the font, size, color, shading, or alignment; add a border or pattern; or format a value for display. Once that's finished, open the **Format** menu and choose **Style**. The Style dialog box contains a list of styles in Excel, including Normal, which is how all cells are formatted initially (boring), along with various style attributes.

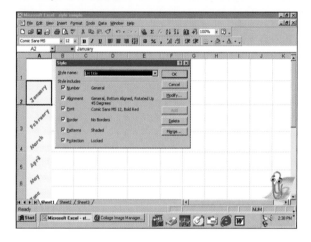

2 Type a New Style Name

Type a brief but descriptive name for the style you just created (the style in the highlighted cell). The cell's formatting is reflected in the Style Includes section of the dialog box; uncheck a box in this section to exclude a specific formatting element from your style. Click **OK** to store the style in the worksheet.

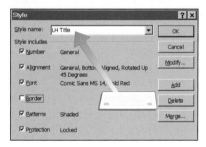

3 Modify Your Style

Styles can be modified after they're created. Choose the style you want to modify from the **Style Name** drop-down list in the Style dialog box and then click the **Modify** button.

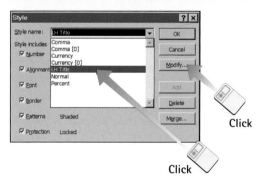

Click

Click

4 Make Changes

The familiar Format Cells dialog box appears. In it, you can change the font, font style, font size, underlining, font color, or effects. Once you've made your selections, click **OK** to close the dialog box.

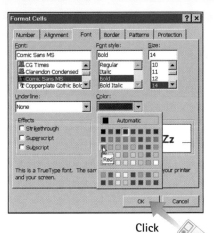

Click

5 Click OK

Click **OK** to save the style and close the Style dialog box. Note that all the cells formatted with that style change in unison when you close the Style dialog box.

End

How-To Hints

Building a Style

The best way to create a style is to format one cell in the worksheet as a sample. Fool around using the Format Cells dialog box. Play. Fiddle. Create. Then open the **Format** menu and choose the **Style** command to put all that effort into one place.

Using the Normal Style

Every cell in the worksheet has a style. Until you create and change the style, Excel gives the cell the Normal style. This uses a rather boring font—Arial 10—which you're probably very sick of by now.

Changing Normal for Good

If you really tire of the Normal font (Arial 10), open the **Tools** menu and choose **Options** to display the Options dialog box. In the **General** tab, choose a new font and size from the Standard Font area. Click **OK**. The change is applied to all your new workbooks as soon as you quit and restart Excel.

Styles Forever

Styles can eventually be a part of something called a *template*, which is like a fill-in-the-blank type of worksheet.

How to Apply Styles

Poor Velma. She's so smart and reads all the latest fashion magazines, but she just doesn't know how to apply styles. For example, she knows all the answers in the make up Dos and Don'ts section, but she still wears blue eye shadow and white lipstick! There's no point in having a style unless you use it.

Creating styles was covered in Task 8. Now it's time to use those styles, applying all the formatting nuggets held within them to various needy and naked cells in your worksheet. Just apply the style to various cells and—Presto!—instant formatting.

Begin

1 Select Cells for a Style

In your document, select cells that you want to instantly format using a style. (Refer to Chapter 3, "Cutting, Copying, and Pasting Information," for more cell selection information.)

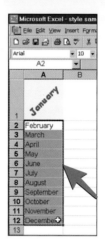

2 Open the Style Dialog Box

Open the **Format** menu and choose **Style**. The Style dialog box displays information about which style is currently applied to the selected cells. That's typically the Normal style, which is as boring as watching continental drift. To choose a different style, click the **down arrow** by the Style Name drop-down list and select the style you prefer. After you select the style, information about it appears in the Style Includes list.

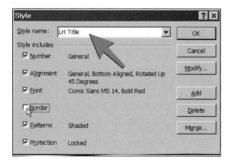

3 Click OK

The selected cells in your document are reformatted to match the style you selected.

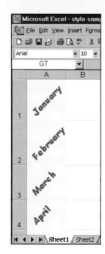

4 Copy Formatting

Excel's **Format Painter** button on the standard toolbar can be used to copy formatting (whether it's a style or not) from one cell to another cell or group of cells. Start by selecting the cell whose format you want to copy.

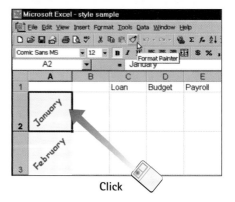

Click

5 Click the Format Painter Button

The selected cell is marked by a line of marching ants; the mouse pointer changes to a plus sign with a paint brush. Excel is ready to copy formatting from the selected cell.

The Format Painter has a hyper mode: It stays active if you double-click the **Format Painter** button. This allows you to point and click at cell after cell to reapply formatting. Press the **Esc** button to end the hyper formatting mode.

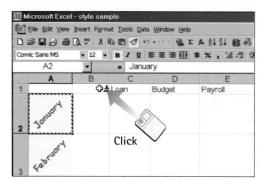

Click

6 Choose the Cell(s) to Format

Click in another cell to apply the selected cell's formatting; alternatively, drag over a row, column, or group of cells to apply the formatting to each one.

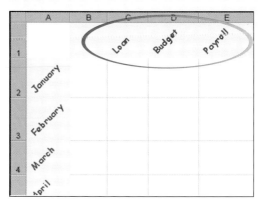

End

How–To Hints

Repeating a Style

If you want to immediately reapply a style to a cell or group of cells in your document, press the **F4** key. The F4 key is the repeat formatting key. If you've just applied the style to cells A1:A6 and notice A7 needs the style too, select **A7** and then press the **F4** key.

Un-Applying a Style

There is really no way to remove formatting from a cell or group of cells. Instead, select the cell(s), open the **Format** menu, choose **Style**, and apply the **Normal** style to the cells. Ugh.

Copy Styles Between Worksheets

To copy a style from one worksheet to another, copy the cell that contains the style in the first worksheet and then open the second worksheet and paste.

How to Automatically Format a Worksheet

Using Excel's AutoFormat tool, you can select a group of cells and pick a format from the list. Excel—all on its own—plucks an interesting and pretty format and applies it in the worksheet.

Begin

1 Select A Group Of Cells

Select a group of cells that you want Excel to automatically format. Excel needs rows and columns of information, so you must select more than one cell. (Excel warns you if you don't.)

2 Open the AutoFormat Dialog Box

Open the **Format** menu and choose **AutoFormat** to open the AutoFormat dialog box.

Click

3 Choose a Sample Style

This dialog box contains a gallery of sample formats, all laid out with color, style, panache, and some exotic spices banned by the FDA. (Click the **Options** button to view the Formats to Apply section that appears at the bottom of the window shown here.) Click one of the samples you like, such as one with enchanting colorful items or maybe one of the alluring 3D samples.

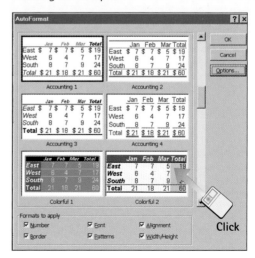

Click

4 Click OK

Wow.

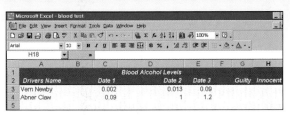

End

How-To Hints

To Remove AutoFormatting

To remove AutoFormatting, select the cells that were AutoFormatted, choose **Format** from the menu, and select **Style**. In the Style dialog box, choose the **Normal** style from the drop-down list and then click **OK**. Bye-bye, fancy stuff!

Another Way to Remove Formatting

You can also remove formatting by choosing the DMV, uh, I mean the **None** option from the list of samples in the AutoFormat dialog box. (None is the last item in the scrolling window.)

Selecting Your Worksheet

If you want to apply AutoFormat to the entire worksheet, do not select it all with Ctrl+A! That selects too much, and it would take hours for everything to get done. Instead, just select the data area (where you've filled in cells with information) by first pressing **Ctrl+Home** and then **Shift+Ctrl+End**. Now use the **AutoFormat** command.

How to Create and Use Templates

Templates in Excel work like outlines or bare-bones worksheets. Basic information, formatting, and formulas are usually entered; the rest of the information is filled out and customized when the template is used. For repetitive forms, templates can be a real time-saver.

Begin

1 Create the Template

Templates are created just like worksheets: You use all the commands to format, insert functions, and lay out the worksheet. The only thing missing is the actual information that varies from worksheet to worksheet.

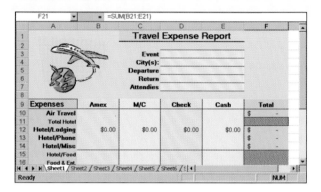

2 Name the Template

Open the **File** menu and choose the **Save As** command. The Save As dialog box opens. Choose **Template** from the **Save as Type** drop-down list; that way the template can be used over and over. Type a name for the template in the File Name field. Be descriptive so you can easily remember what template you made. I've typed Travel Report.

3 Save in the XLSTART Folder

Excel templates work best when all of them are saved in a specific spot on disk—the XLSTART folder. (Every template in this folder is displayed in the New dialog box when you go to open a new workbook in Excel.) To save your new template in this folder, open the **Save As** dialog box's **Save In** drop-down list; click the icon representing your PC's hard drive, click the **Windows** entry, choose **Application Data**, **Microsoft**, **Excel**, and then click **XLSTART**. Click **Save**. The template is saved to disk.

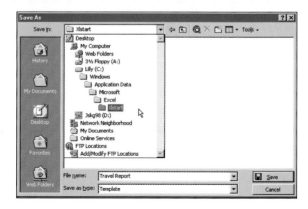

4 Close the Template

Choose **Close** from the **File** menu to close the template. If you don't close the template, any changes you make to it will be reflected in the template, not in a new worksheet.

Click

5 Make a New Worksheet

In Excel, open the **File** menu and choose **New**. The New dialog box displays any templates that you have created, along with a generic Workbook template. Double-click the template you want to use to create a worksheet.

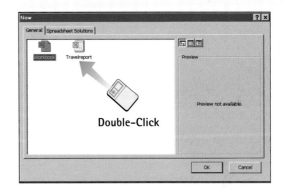

Double-Click

6 Enter Data in the Worksheet

A new worksheet that is based on your template opens. From here on, progress continues just as it normally would in Excel, although you have a lot of work already done for you. Don't forget to save the workbook to disk!

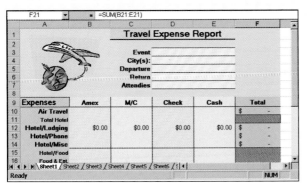

End

How-To Hints

Building a Template

One of the best ways to create a template is to first create a real worksheet, such as an invoice or report. Remove the information that changes each time you print and save that worksheet as a template to use over and over.

Editing a Template

To modify an existing template, open the **File** menu and select **Open** instead of New. That way you open the template for editing and don't use the template to create a new worksheet.

Use the File, New Command

Notice that only the **File, New** command summons the New dialog box to use a template. Neither **Ctrl+N** nor the **New** toolbar button displays the New dialog box.

Task

CHAPTER 7

Charts and Graphs

*T*hey say that no one has ever been hit by a bus they saw coming. How true; surprises will get you every time, but you can react if you know what's coming.

This is where spreadsheets can come in handy: They let you examine data and help you use that data to predict when you're about to get hit by a bus (figuratively, of course). For example, looking at this year's monthly income might tell you that everything is hunky-dory, but you might notice a subtle decline when you compare it with the previous three-years' income.

While you could run a series of what-ifs in a worksheet, adjusting values to see how they affect other values, a better way is to look at your information differently—in a chart or a graph. Charts are one way of showing the clueless and non-visionary what the numbers really *mean*. While a worksheet may be a thing to behold, only by creating a nifty pie chart or line graph can you show the boss what the numbers really mean. While the boss marvels at how pretty the chart is, you can explain things, like "Hey! We've got a bus coming!" ●

How to Use the Chart Wizard

When Aladdin rubbed the magic lamp, the genie announced that he could grant only three wishes. Oh, joy. But three wishes from a genie can't really compare to the infinite number of requests from a wizard—especially if it's Excel's magical Chart Wizard.

Ah, the wonderful wizard of charts. Back in the olden days, *charts* (which, in Excel, means any type of graph) were created in Excel using stone tablets and chisels. We've come a long way. Today, creating a chart is a snap.

Begin

1 Select Data to Graph

The Chart Wizard requires information, usually in the form of cells containing values. The cells can be in a row, column, or table. (Tables are specifically covered in Task 6.) Select the information you want to graph (including headers, if applicable).

	A	B	C	D	E	F	G	H	I
1			INSPECTING CAROL DEMOGRAPHICS						
2	Date	Season Tkts	Adults	Students	Sr.Citizens	Children	Comps	Walk-Ins	Total
3	Dec. 4	30	17	5	13	3	14	17	99
4	Dec. 5	14	18	1	2	3	1	21	60
5	Dec. 6	0	0	0	0	0	0	0	0
6	Dec. 10	7	21	37	5	1	2	5	78
7	Dec. 11	24	14	7	11	0	5	6	67
8	Dec. 12	14	134	11	8	6	5	6	184
9	Dec. 13	21	25	1	8	7	9	5	76
10	Dec. 17	4	16	5	6	1	9	8	49
11	Dec. 18	12	22	1	6	1	13	12	67
12	Dec. 19	14	41	11	12	4	20	22	124
13									
14	TOTAL:	140	308	79	71	26	78	102	804
15									
16									

2 Start the Chart Wizard

Click the **Chart Wizard** button (see step 1). Select the type of chart you want from the Chart Wizard's first screen. Choose a chart category from the list box from the left side of the **Standard Types** tab, and then select a chart type from the window on the right. (Click the **Custom Types** tab for even more chart types.) I've chosen to create a pie chart. To view a sample of the chart category and type you selected, click and hold the **Press and Hold to View Sample** button. When you're satisfied with your selections, click **Next**.

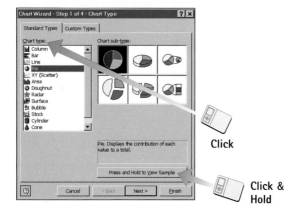

Click

Click & Hold

3 Specify Source Data

Use the Chart Wizard's second screen to view what your chart looks like so far (a line graph is displayed in this example) and tweak your source data. If you're graphing information from a table, you can reorient the table using the Rows or Columns button. You can also use the Data Range field to add cells to the range, or click the button to the right of the Data Range field to reselect the cells you want to chart. (This feature works best with tables rather than rows or columns of data.) Click **Next** to continue.

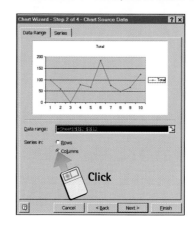

Click

4 Set Chart Options

You can use the various tabs in the wizard's third screen to name the chart and its components, set the chart's axes, fiddle with the gridlines, establish a chart legend, label the data, and more. It's best to work through each part of the dialog box to see what the various steps do to your chart. This is a visual thing. When you're satisfied with your selections, click **Next**.

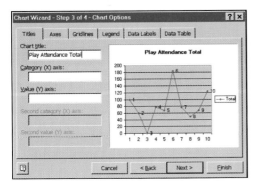

5 Specify the Chart Location

You finally get to decide whether you want the new chart to be a separate sheet in your workbook or have it appear as an object in the worksheet. We recommend that large charts be in their own sheet. Smaller charts fit in nicely with the present worksheet's information.

6 Click Finish

The chart is created either in the current worksheet or on a separate sheet. If it's a separate sheet, you'll see the chart appear in Chart 1 along with Sheet 1 and other tabs at the bottom of Excel's window. In addition, the Chart palette appears, allowing you to further customize the chart.

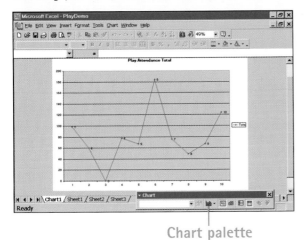

Chart palette

End

How-To Hints

Graphing Information in a Table

If you're charting information in a table, be certain of what graph type you're creating. Some graphs lend themselves well to tables, but other graphs look tacky. Also, be sure to select the headings (if any) around the table so that the Chart Wizard places that information into the chart.

When Can I Click Finish?

Though there are four steps in the Chart Wizard, you can click the **Finish** button any time you like; Excel puts the chart into the worksheet with whatever settings you established. (Excel "assumes" the rest of the settings.) Remember: You can always edit the chart later.

Printing the Chart

Charts print best when you create them as separate sheets inside the workbook. Otherwise, when you go to print your worksheet, open the View menu and choose **Page Break Preview** to ensure that the chart won't be sliced between two pages. If the preview indicates that the chart will be broken, move the chart to its own page.

Updating the Chart

Charts in Excel are *live*. If you change the data in your worksheet, the chart changes accordingly—and instantly. It's fun to watch.

How to Create a Bar Graph

Bar graphs are the most popular type of spreadsheet graph—probably because most accountants spend too much time in bars.

Oh, ha ha.

Seriously, bar graphs are nice because they compare values in a series, such as months or days. They have a solid feel to them. For example, "income" just looks better as a solid bar as opposed to a skimpy line wiggling up and down a grid. Of course, the decision on what type of chart you make is always up to you.

Begin

1 Select Cells to Graph

The cells should contain information you want to put into a chart. Your selection can be a series of cells in a row or column, or an entire table (see Task 6). If the cells have a heading describing their values, select it as well.

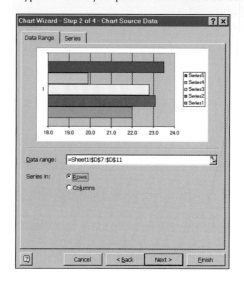

2 Start the Chart Wizard

Open the Insert menu and choose **Chart**. There are several types of bar graphs shown in the Chart Wizard. Choose a type (**Bar** is chosen here); then choose a subtype. To preview the chart you've selected, click and hold the **Press and Hold to View Sample** button. Click **Next** when you're satisfied with your selection.

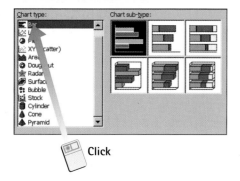

Click

3 Fiddle with the Source Data

In the wizard's second screen, confirm that you have the proper cells selected for the graph and that they're in the right columns. Consider playing with the **Rows** and **Columns** buttons to see which type of chart you prefer. Click **Next** to continue.

4 Name Your Chart

Add a title to your chart by clicking the **Titles** tab and entering the title in the **Chart Title** box. Optionally, title the X and Y axes. (Feel free to play with other items in this screen.) Click **Next** to continue.

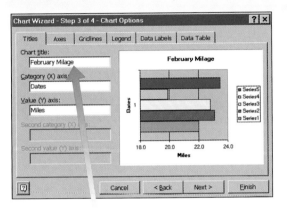

5 Set the Chart Location

If you change your mind about options set in previous screens, click **Back** to change your information. Otherwise, decide whether to create the chart as a new sheet in the workbook or just plop it down as an object in the current worksheet.

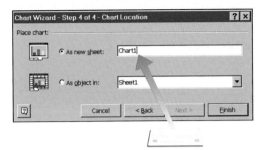

6 Click Finish

The new chart appears either in your worksheet as an object or in a sheet all on its own (depending on which option you selected in step 5).

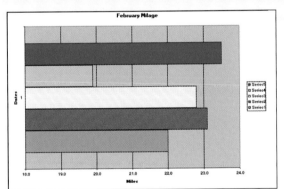

End

How-To Hints

Repositioning the Chart

A chart in a worksheet is its own object. You can click it to select it or drag it around using the mouse.

Resizing the Chart

To change the chart's size, begin by clicking it. Eight black handles appear on the chart's sides and corners. Drag them in or out to readjust the size. If you press the **Shift** key and drag a corner, you can uniformly change the chart's size.

Oops! Wrong Bar Graph

You notice that Phil over in Accounting prefers the 3D style of bar graphs. No problem! Right-click the graph part of your chart. Choose **Chart Type** from the pop-up menu. This displays the Chart Type dialog box, from which you can choose another type of chart for your data.

How to Create a Pie Chart

After a big meal of raw data and number crunching, nothing beats a pie chart for dessert. Pie charts are fun because they're round. I'm serious! Bar charts are boring to look at; so are line charts and any other type of chart. For some reason, people love looking at pie charts. *USA Today* couldn't be published without one!

Pie charts are most useful for displaying information in terms of portions of a whole—for example, spending by department, income by source, or types of cars driven. Even two-part data looks good in a pie chart: males versus females, winter versus summer, or yea verses nay.

The best type of data to fold into a pie chart is serial: information in a row or column. You can choose any number of cells, from two to a zillion—but don't select a table! (Instead, select totals from the table.)

Begin

1 Start the Chart Wizard

Once you've selected the data you want to fold into a pie chart, open the Insert menu and choose **Chart**. The Chart Wizard's first screen comes forward, displaying a palette full of chart choices. Select **Pie** from the **Chart Type** list, and then select the type of pie chart you want to use from the **Chart Sub-Type** area. Click and hold the **Press and Hold to View Sample** button to preview the chart you've selected. Click **Next** when you're satisfied with your selection.

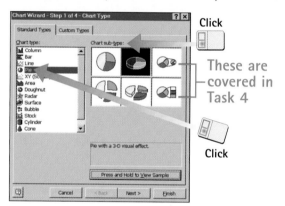

Click

These are covered in Task 4

Click

2 Add a Title

The Chart Wizard's second screen shows you a preview of your pie chart; click **Next** to advance to the third screen, where you can add various chart features, including a chart title. To add a title, click the **Titles** tab and type it into the Chart Title field. Note that the title you type appears in the preview window.

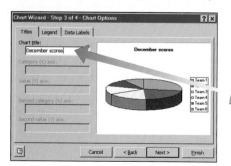

3 Enter Legend Information

Click the **Legend** tab. To turn the legend display on or off, click the **Show Legend** check box. Use the radio buttons in the Placement area to specify where you want the legend to appear in relation to the chart. Note that the data that appears in the legend in the preview window was taken from the original worksheet. Click **Next** to continue.

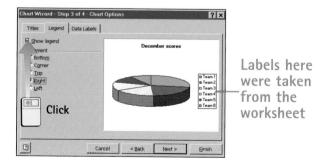

Labels here were taken from the worksheet

Click

4 Label Your Data

Data labels allow you to apply meaning (such as percentages) to the items in your chart. To experiment, choose **Show Percent** and see how it affects your chart. Other values display different types of labels on the chart. Click **Next** to continue.

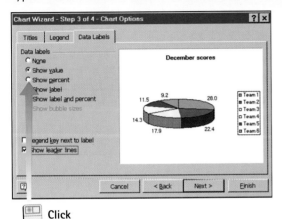

Click

5 Set the Chart Location

Decide whether you want the new chart to appear as an object in the worksheet or on a sheet by itself.

Click

6 Click Finish

Ah! There it is, a wondrous pie chart.

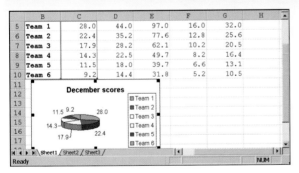

End

How-To Hints

Pie Too Small?

You can change the size of the pie chart by right-clicking it and choosing **Chart Type** from the pop-up menu. (You're clicking on the wrong spot if that command isn't on the pop-up menu; try again.)

Too Many Slices?

If your pie has too many slices—especially a fanfold of very small slices—consider creating a pie-of-pie or bar-of-pie type of chart (see Task 4).

Changing a Pie Chart Angle

To change the position at which Excel begins drawing the pie, right-click **Pie** in the final chart and choose **Format Data Series** from the pop-up menu. Enter the angle for the first slice in the **Options** tab of the Format Data Series dialog box. The pie chart is reformatted to begin the first slice at the angle you specified.

How to Create an Exploding Pie Chart

Much to our severe disappointment, an exploding pie chart doesn't actually explode. Microsoft obviously wasn't clever enough to have tiny fireworks shooting off the pie, or sounds of crackling and popping. No, they just weren't thinking.

Truth be known, that's because you use an exploding pie chart not when you want one piece to disappear, but rather when you want to separate a piece of information for recognition of some sort. You can add a note saying, "My piece is bigger" or "Honey, you spent too much here!"

Begin

1 Start the Chart Wizard

Select a series of cells in a row or column (along with their headings), or an entire table. Then start the Chart Wizard by opening the **Insert** menu and choosing **Chart**. In the wizard's **Chart Type** screen, select **Pie** from the **Chart type** list and then select either the first or second pie in the **Chart Sub-Type** area. (Choosing either of the preset exploding pie types creates a pie with every piece exploded; the steps in this task are for exploding only one piece.) Click **Next** to continue.

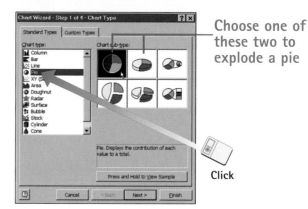

Choose one of these two to explode a pie

Click

2 Click Next

No changes are necessary in the Chart Wizard's second and third screens, so click **Next** in both dialog boxes to advance to the Chart Location screen. Choosing **As Object In** places your pie smack in the middle of your worksheet. If your pie is small and your information short, you may like this. If you want to make a big impression and use additional information, **As New Sheet** may be a better choice. Whatever you decide, click **Finish** to close the wizard and view your pie.

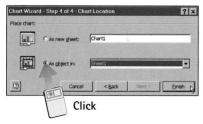

Click

3 Shrink the Pie

Your pie is probably too large to really explode it; you'll probably want to shrink it. Click once on your pie to select it; this attaches little handles to the pie chart. Click once outside the pie circle to add a gray Plot Area square. Click a corner handle and drag toward the middle of the pie to shrink it. (Do the same with the legend if you prefer.)

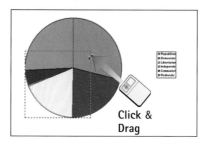

Click & Drag

4 Explode a Slice

Select the slice that you want to explode from the chart—you may have to click a few times before you select only one slice of the pie. Handles outline the slice you've selected; click a handle and drag the slice out and away from the pie's center. (You can drag only to the edge of the sheet.) Release the mouse and—pop!—you've exploded only one piece of pie. Note that information about the pie slice appears in a pop-up box when the mouse hovers over the slice.

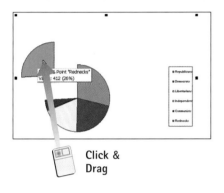

Click & Drag

5 Insert a Callout

Adding a callout isn't necessary, but if you're going to explode a piece of your pie, you might as well draw more attention to it and explain its significance. To insert a callout, click the **AutoShapes** button on the Drawing toolbar, choose **Callouts**, and then select the shape you want your callout to assume.

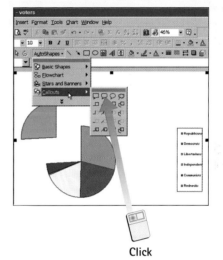

Click

6 Draw Your Callout

When the cursor changes to a plus sign, drag the mouse to position the callout in your chart and then type the callout's text inside the space you've drawn. If the text runs too short or too long, you can re-size the callout by clicking it and dragging one of the handles.

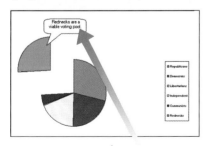

How-To Hints

Enlarging Your Legend
To enlarge your legend, single-click to select it and then click and drag the handles as needed.

Enlarging Your Legend Text
To enlarge the text in your legend, click the legend to select it, click the **Font Size** box, and select a larger font size.

Bringing Out the Drawing Toolbar
Choose **View, Toolbars, Drawing** to display the drawing toolbar.

End

How to Create a Pie-of-Pie Chart

You have your various pie flavors. There's pie-in-the-sky and pie-in-your-face and pie á là mode, then along comes that mathematical thing, pi (π). And now pie-of-pie?

Fear ye not! You've probably seen lots of pie-of-pie charts in your travels. A *pie-of-pie chart* is simply a regular pie chart with a fanfold of very tiny slices. Those slices are then exploded into their own mini pie charts, sitting right next to the big guy. That's all it is.

Begin

1 Start the Chart Wizard

The data for a pie-of-pie chart should be a single row or column. A pie-of-pie chart typically has several larger values in a series and a whole cluster of small values as well. Select them all and then start the Chart Wizard by opening the **Insert** menu and choosing **Chart**. Select **Pie** from the **Chart Type** list and then choose either the **pie-of-pie** or **bar-of-pie** (which displays a little bar instead of a little pie for the tiny values) subtype. Click **Next**.

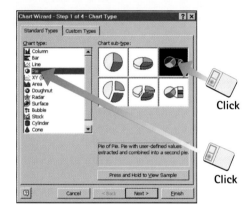

Click

Click

2 Enter Chart Options

Preview your chart, and click **Next** to set your chart options. You can enter a title for your chart in the **Titles** tab of the Chart Options dialog; you can also display labels by each pie slice. There are several options in the dialog box. Choose each one to see what it affects. Don't worry if things look crowded; it can be fixed later. Click **Next**.

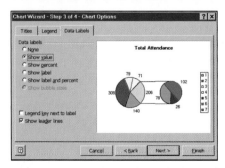

3 Set the Chart Location

You're now in the Chart Location dialog box. Choose **As New Sheet** to have the pie-of-pie chart appear as a new chart sheet in your workbook. If you choose **As Object In**, the chart becomes an object in the current worksheet. Either way, click **Finish** to view your chart.

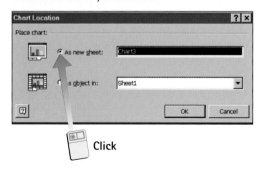

Click

4 Tweak the Sub-Pie

The pie-of-pie chart appears, displaying your data in a format where the small values don't get overlooked. If you're not happy with the number of items in the *sub-pie* (the pie showing the smaller values), right-click either pie in the chart and choose **Format Data Series** from the pop-up menu.

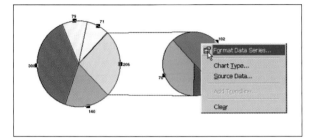

5 Click the Options Tab

Use the settings Format Data Series dialog box's Options tab to change the way the sub-pie looks. For example, adjust the number of items in the sub-pie by clicking the arrows in the **Second Plot Contains the Last** spin box; change the size of the sub-pie by clicking the arrows in the **Size of Second Plot** spin box; set the distance between two pies by clicking the arrows in the **Gap Width** spin box.

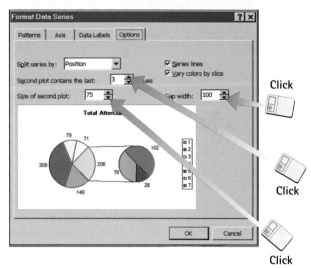

Click

Click

Click

6 Click OK

The pie is changed according to your specifications.

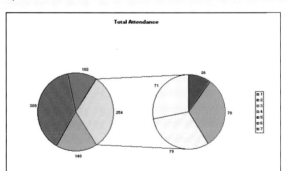

End

How-To Hints

Pie-of-Pie Graphing a Table

You really can't create a pie-of-pie graph of information in a table—it just doesn't work. Instead, graph the table's summary or the sum of each row or column.

What About Pie-of-Pie-of-Pie?

Excel doesn't do pie-of-pie-of-pie. If your data is that bad, consider rewriting it in the worksheet so that very, very tiny values are lumped together; then do a separate pie chart for those values.

How to Put a Table into a Chart

Graphs can inspire chills of delight or of fear; complex graphs can lead to information glut. For example, it's too easy to select a whole table of numbers, start the Chart Wizard, and just print out the results. Sure, it's a chart—but what does it say?

When you're charting an entire table, care should be taken so that the information doesn't look bulky and awkward in the graph. Where possible, you should summarize totals or provide separate charts of the details. Otherwise, follow along with the task to create the best possible graph for your table.

Begin

1 Start the Chart Wizard

Select the table you want to chart—title, headings, and all. (Excel uses that information when it labels the chart.) Start the Chart Wizard by opening the Insert menu and choosing **Chart**. Select **Column** from the **Chart Type** list and choose from the available subtypes. Certain subtypes lend themselves to handling information in tables—the 3D column chart, for example. Click **Next**.

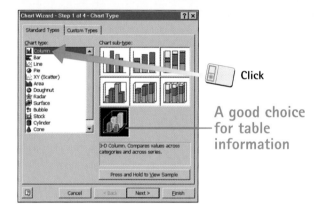

Click

A good choice for table information

2 Preview Your Chart

Preview your chart. (Consider switching between the **Rows** and **Columns** radio buttons to see which perspective you like best.) Notice that the labels show up in the preview if you properly labeled your table.

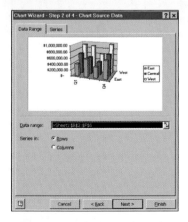

3 Complete the Wizard

You can use the Chart Options dialog box in the wizard's third screen to add a title, labels, or other chart features, but be warned: Using too many of these options can make the chart look too crowded. That's definitely not what you want. Click **Next** and then decide whether to put the final product on its own separate sheet in the workbook or as an object in the current worksheet; click **Finish**.

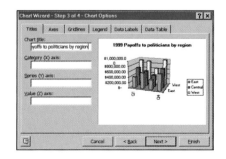

4 Tweak Your Chart

Lo, there's your chart! Sometimes the angle at which the chart is shown obscures information. You can change your viewing angle easily with a 3D bar type of chart; simply right-click the chart and choose **3D View** from the pop-up menu.

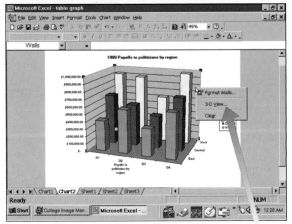

Click

5 Fiddle with 3D Options

The 3-D View dialog box enables you to rotate the chart to the perfect angle. Use the **Elevation** buttons (in the top left) and text box to change the height from which you view the image, and use the **Rotation** text box and buttons (immediately below the preview image) to change the left and right angles. Zoom in or out on the image using the **Perspective** buttons (to the right of the preview image) and text box. Click the **Apply** button to see your chart change without exiting the dialog box; click **Default** to restore the chart if you've goofed around too much.

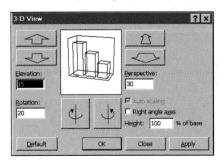

6 Click OK

Your chart has been adjusted.

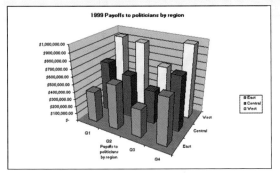

End

How-To Hints

How Tall Is That Building?

A table chart is often hard to read, especially when there is lots of information in tall bars resembling downtown buildings. To find the specific value of any bar in the chart, point the mouse at that bar (don't click!). A pop-up bubble appears, explaining what the bar represents and its value.

Getting Rid of a Title

Getting rid of any element in a chart is simple: Click once to select it and then press the **Delete** key. If the information is part of a series (bars, values, and so on), click again to select an individual element in the series and then delete it.

How to Change a Chart

Choices, choices, choices. Can too many choices spoil a good thing, or does it just give too much power to the indecisive? For example, every McDonald's in the land has almost the same menu. Why do some people stare at it for so long trying to decide what to order? And why wasn't that decision made earlier in the line?

But we're getting sidetracked again. With charts in Excel, you can always change your mind. Any number of things in a chart can be changed subject to your whim—and without the blistering effect of other people in line staring at your back.

Begin

1 Change the Chart Type

Don't seethe with jealousy because you chose the wrong type of chart. Change it! Right-click the graph inside the chart object or on the chart sheet and then choose **Chart Type** from the pop-up menu.

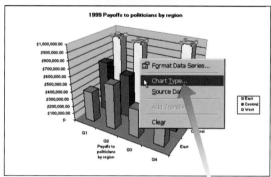

Click

2 Pick a Different Type

The Chart Type dialog box contains the same list of types and subtypes you saw when using the Chart Wizard. Select a chart type from the list and then decide upon a subtype.

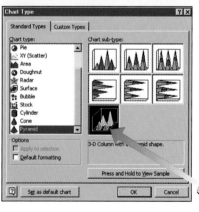

Click

3 Click OK

The chart—and the information in the chart—changes to reflect the chart you chose in step 2.

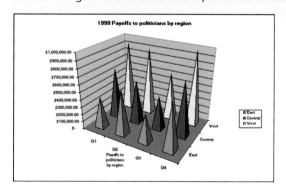

4 Change a Chart's Colors

To change a chart's colors, begin by clicking the portion of the chart whose colors you want to change. You must be precise here—click exactly on the part of the graph you want to change. Black resizing handles appear on the selected item(s). Right-click the selected area and choose either **Format Data Point** or **Format Data Series** from the pop-up menu. (**Format Data Point** appears when you've selected a single item in a graph, while **Format Data Series** appears when you've select a row of data from a table graph.)

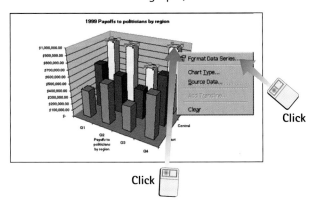

Click

Click

5 Click the Patterns Tab

Now select the **Patterns** tab of the **Format Data Series** dialog box (the **Format Data Point** dialog box if you're formatting a single item in the graph). Select various settings in order to change the color or line style for that part of the graph. Choose from the **Color** area to set the fill color and click **Fill Effects** to select from a variety of fill features.

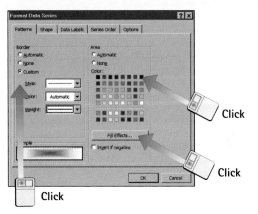

Click

Click

Click

6 Click OK

Your chart is updated with the proper color settings.

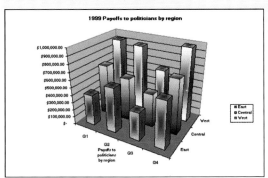

End

How-To Hints

Changing Walls and Floors

You can change the color of just about any part of a chart: Just right-click and choose the top item from the pop-up menu. That displays a dialog box from which you can reassign colors or patterns for whatever you right-clicked in the chart.

Modifying the Legend

The chart's legend uses information from your worksheet. If the legend is boring, it's probably because your worksheet lacks information describing the chart. To fix it, right-click the chart and choose **Source Data**. Select the cells containing the chart's data as well as label information in your worksheet. The legend grows labels when you click **OK**.

Changing a Chart's Data

The information graphed in a chart comes from cells in a spreadsheet. Change the cells to change the chart. We're not advocating cooking the books, but any information changed in a worksheet changes the graph made from those cells.

Task

8

Preparing the Document

What is a document? There is a certain mental image everyone comes up with when you say "the word," but what is it really? A *document* is communication or information on paper. It's a way of expressing something. Although "document" usually refers to something formal or official, little Miranda's crayon doodles could be considered "documents" as well—though only a psychologist would refer to them that way.

The idea behind the document is really to make your mark, to communicate or express yourself to others. Leaving your mark is important, and it's equally important that the mark you leave carries the weight it's due.

Printing from a computer is usually the final result of creating a document—the "leaving your mark" part. First you create and experiment, then you format, then you print (and, of course, all along you save). All that work and effort should be reflected on the hard copy, the printed page, the document.

With printing come a lot of other issues. For example, the printed information may need to have page numbers and margins. Also, previewing your printing helps ensure that information doesn't get "orphaned" on a second page or that graphics or a chart aren't split between two pages. Excel makes all this easy. ●

How to Zoom In and Out

"Momma, why are those cars so small?" Simon asks. We answer, "We're in an airplane and we're far away from them. And, if for some reason the plane's engines go out, we'll go *zooming* towards those cars and they'll get bigger and bigger until we get too close..."

Zooming in and out in your document is the same thing as getting closer and farther away from your work. It's as easy as a click of a button or two to view your work at different sizes, and it all happens without the danger of plunging 35,000 feet into some cars.

Begin

1 Open the Zoom Dialog Box

Click the **View** menu and choose **Zoom** to open the Zoom dialog box. This dialog box enables you to specify whether you want to view your document at 100% (the "real-life" size, or as best as can be approximated on your screen), or whether you want items in your document to appear larger or smaller. Large values (such as 200%) zoom in, making your worksheet appear larger, while small values (such as 25%) zoom out, making your worksheet appear smaller. Select one of the **Magnification** radio buttons (or enter a custom size in the Custom field).

Click

2 Click OK

The screen is *zoomed* to the new magnification.

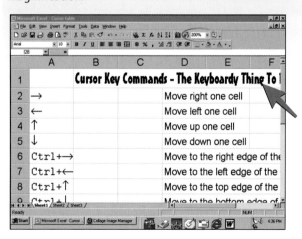

3 Click the Zoom Box

You can click the **Zoom** box on the standard toolbar to quickly zoom in or out on your text. To enter a number instead of selecting one from the list, click in the box and type any value between 10 and 400.

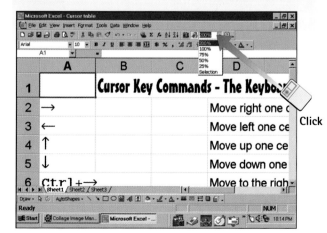

Click

4 Zoom In on Selected Items

Excel gives you the option of zooming in on selected items; that way your screen literally becomes filled with the cell or group of cells you've selected. Begin by selecting the cells you want to fill your screen.

	1999 Mileage Log			
Date	Starting	Ending	Total	Trip
1-Jan		12575.2		
5-Jan	12575.2	12597.2	22.0	Bank
26-Jan	12634.2	12659.2	25.0	Bank/FedX
Total for January			47.0	
4-Feb	12701.0	12723.0	22.0	FedX
9-Feb	12776.0	12799.1	23.1	Bank
17-Feb	12852.1	12874.9	22.8	Bank
28-Feb	12927.9	12947.8	9	PO
23-Feb	13000.8	13024.3	23.5	
Total for February			111.3	
2-Mar	13057.8	13082.7	24.9	Bank/FedX
5-Mar	13129.9	13153.5	23.6	FedX

5 Click the Zoom Box

Click the **down arrow** next to the Zoom box and choose **Selection** from the drop-down list.

	A	B	C	D	E	F
1		1999 Mileage Log				
2	Date	Starting	Ending	Total	Trip	
3	1-Jan		12575.2			
4	5-Jan	12575.2	12597.2	22.0	Bank	
5	26-Jan	12634.2	12659.2	25.0	Bank/FedX	
6	Total for January			47.0		
7	4-Feb	12701.0	12723.0	22.0	FedX	
8	9-Feb	12776.0	12799.1	23.1	Bank	
9	17-Feb	12852.1	12874.9	22.8	Bank	
10	28-Feb	12927.9	12947.8	19.9	PO	
11	23-Feb	13000.8	13024.3	23.5	Bank	
12	Total for February			111.3		
13	2-Mar	13057.8	13082.7	24.9	Bank/FedX	
14	5-Mar	13129.9	13153.5	23.6	FedX	

Click

6 View the Results

Your screen is filled with the cells you selected. (To zoom out, choose **100%** from the **Zoom** box.)

	A	B	C	D
6	Total for January			47.0
7	4-Feb	12701.0	12723.0	22.0
8	9-Feb	12776.0	12799.1	23.1
9	17-Feb	12852.1	12874.9	22.8
10	28-Feb	12927.9	12947.8	19.9
11	23-Feb	13000.8	13024.3	23.5

End

How-To Hints

Zooming Is a Visual Thing

When you zoom, it's as though you're using a magnifying glass to make your worksheet appear larger or smaller. Just as when you use a magnifying glass, you're not changing what you're looking at, but merely how you see it—unless you use the **Zoom** command outside in the sun, in which case the focused sunlight can burn a hole in the line of ants used to select a cell.

Zooming Doesn't Affect Printing

Regardless of how big or small you've zoomed your document, it still prints at 100%.

How to Split the Screen

Documents, such as a loan spreadsheet, can be pretty long. A five-year loan with monthly payments gives your worksheet lots of rows. Viewing both the beginning and the ending of your document at the same time is easy: Just split the screen. Luckily, this doesn't involve knives or sharp tools other than those found in Excel.

Begin

1 Find the Split Boxes

At the top of the vertical scrollbar and to the right of the horizontal scrollbar are what are called *split boxes*. Use the vertical split box (at the top of the vertical scrollbar) to split your screen so that you have top and bottom windows; use the horizontal split box (to the right of the horizontal scrollbar) to split your screen so that you have left and right windows.

2 Drag the Split

When you point at a split box, the mouse pointer changes to a two-headed arrow. Click and drag the split box until the screen is split where you want it. When you release the split box, you'll see two windows, each with its own scrollbars. That means you can look at two different parts of your document at once; just scroll to the spot you need in each window. If you want to split the screen again to view four parts of your document at once, drag the other tab in.

3 Select a Cell

There's another way to quarter your screen. First, remove the split(s) you set in steps 1 and 2 by double-clicking the split line or by dragging it to the edge of your worksheet. Second, click any cell.

Click

4 Quarter the Screen

Open the **Window** menu and choose **Split** to divide your screen into four sections. (To remove the split, open the **Window** menu and choose **Remove Split**.)

	A	B	C	D	E	F	G
1	THE LOAN MACHINE						
2		Loan Amount	$ 26,000.00		Total paid	$56,420.19	
3		Term (years)	6		Total Interest	$29,647.31	
4		Interest Rate	21.00%				
5	Date	Balance	Payment	Principal	Interest		
6	Jan-99	$ 26,000.00	$772.88	$134.94	($637.94)		
7	Feb-99	$ 25,865.06	$772.88	$138.25	($634.62)		
8	Mar-99	$ 25,726.80	$772.88	$141.65	($631.23)		
9	Apr-99	$ 25,585.16	$772.88	$145.12	($627.76)		
10	May-99	$ 25,440.03	$772.88	$148.68	($624.20)		
11	Jun-99	$ 25,291.35	$772.88	$152.33	($620.55)		
12	Jul-99	$ 25,139.02	$772.88	$156.07	($616.81)		
13	Aug-99	$ 24,982.95	$772.88	$159.90	($612.98)		
14	Sep-99	$ 24,823.05	$772.88	$163.82	($609.06)		
15	Oct-99	$ 24,659.23	$772.88	$167.84	($605.04)		

5 Freeze Panes

Splitting a window is nice, but consider freezing the panes for a long-term solution. This is handy if you have a huge table and want to keep the headers in view (without the bother of an ugly split bar). Begin by splitting (or quartering) the window using the steps outlined earlier. (For a table, select the cell just below the header row and to the right of the leftmost column, and choose **Split** from the Window menu.) Open the **Window** menu and choose **Freeze Panes**. The document looks unchanged, but darker lines mark where the splits once were.

	A	B	C	D	E	F	G
1	THE LOAN MACHINE						
2		Loan Amount	$ 26,000.00		Total paid	$56,420.19	
3		Term (years)	6		Total Interest	$29,647.31	
4		Interest Rate	21.00%				
5	Date	Balance	Payment	Principal	Interest		
6	Jan-99	$ 26,000.00	$772.88	$134.94	($637.94)		
7	Feb-99	$ 25,865.06	$772.88	$138.25	($634.62)		
8	Mar-99	$ 25,726.80	$772.88	$141.65	($631.23)		
9	Apr-99	$ 25,585.16	$772.88	$145.12	($627.76)		
10	May-99	$ 25,440.03	$772.88	$148.68	($624.20)		
11	Jun-99	$ 25,291.35	$772.88	$152.33	($620.55)		
12	Jul-99	$ 25,139.02	$772.88	$156.07	($616.81)		
13	Aug-99	$ 24,982.95	$772.88	$159.90	($612.98)		
14	Sep-99	$ 24,823.05	$772.88	$163.82	($609.06)		
15	Oct-99	$ 24,659.23	$772.88	$167.84	($605.04)		

6 Unfreeze Panes

To unfreeze any panes in your document, open the **Windows** menu and choose **Unfreeze Panes**. Then open the **Window** menu a second time, and select **Remove Split** to get rid of the split bars that appear.

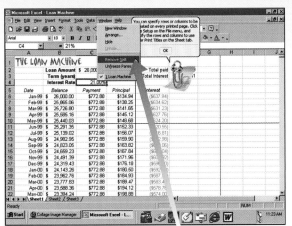

Click

How-To Hints

Moving the Split Box

If you drag the split line itself (not the split box), you move it one cell at a time within the worksheet. If you double-click the split box (instead of dragging it), Excel splits your worksheet right down the middle (the middle of what you can see).

I Can't Split!

When you use the Freeze Panes command, Excel no longer lets you use the Split command. This is true even if you've frozen only one pane.

Printing Frozen Panes

What if your worksheet prints page after page and ignores any row or column headers you may have frozen? To prevent that, open the **File** menu and choose **Page Setup**. You can select rows or columns from the Sheet tab that you want to have appear at the top of every printed sheet.

End

How to Add Headers and Footers

A printed document can be more than just the information in your worksheet. For example, a multipage document might need page numbers; maybe you should add a header that displays the document's name or other information. Excel is capable of that, providing you know which buttons to push.

Begin

1 Open the Page Setup Dialog Box

Click the **View** menu and choose **Header and Footer**. The Page Setup dialog box appears; it contains a ton of controls for the final document, most of which deal with printing. Use the **Header/Footer** tab to set a header or footer for the document.

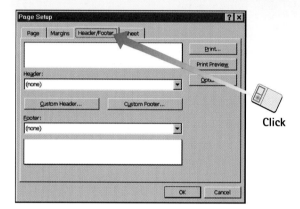

Click

2 Choose a Predefined Header

Click the **down arrow** by the Header field to view the Header drop-down list. (Many of the items in this list relate to the document's name, your name, the computer name, the current date and time, and so on.) Choose a predefined header from the list. The space above the list shows you how it will look on the final, printed document. (If you don't want a header, choose **(none)**.)

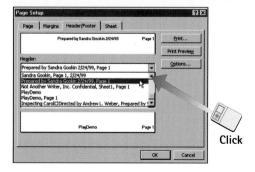

Click

3 Choose a Predefined Footer

Click the **down arrow** by the Footer field to display the Footer drop-down list. Either choose a predefined footer from the list or choose **(none)** if you don't want one. The preview window below the drop-down list shows you how the footer will look on the final, printed document.

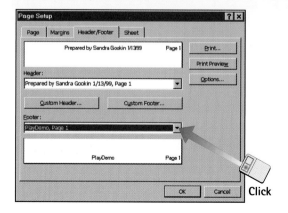

Click

4 Set a Customized Header/Footer

To roll your own header or footer, click either the **Custom Header** or **Custom Footer** button. A dialog box appears; it is identical for both buttons. Use the controls in the dialog box to build your header or footer, placing text or secret commands into the Left, Center, or Right sections.

Font dialog box / Insert total pages in document / Insert current time

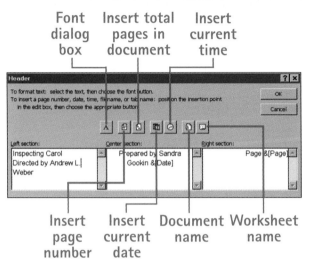

Insert page number / Insert current date / Document name / Worksheet name

5 View the Results

Click **OK** once in the Header or Footer dialog box and again in the Page Setup dialog box. View the results of your efforts by either printing the final document or opening the **File** menu and choosing the **Print Preview** command.

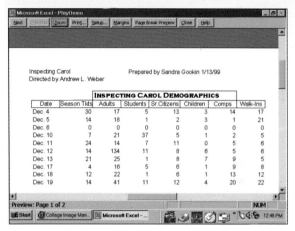

End

How-To Hints

Here's Page Setup Again!
You can also access the Page Setup dialog box by selecting the **Page Setup** command from the **File** menu. Click the **Header/Footer** tab to create a header, a footer, or both.

Viewing the Header/Footer
You can view the header or footer without printing by using the **Print Preview** command (see Task 5).

Use Those Fonts!
Use the custom Header or Footer dialog box to change the fonts Excel automatically assigns to your header or footer. Select the text in the Left, Right, or Center section and then click the **Font** button (the one with an **A** on it). This summons a Font dialog box. Be creative.

Header and Footer Margins
Excel sets special margins for the header and footer; they're different from the standard margins around the page. See Task 4 for more information on setting header and footer margins.

How to Adjust Your Margins

If you've come here trying to adjust margins when buying stocks or bonds, you're in the wrong place. Sure, spreadsheets are about the money game, but margins aren't only for the stock market. Margins also exist around printed pages. There are left, right, top, and bottom margins, which Excel lets you adjust to your whim. Sure, they mean nothing until you print. But before you do print a document, you might want to check the margins to ensure they're doing the job they're meant to do—keeping your printed stuff from looking too close to the edge of the page.

Begin

1 Open the Page Setup Dialog Box

Click the **File** menu and choose **Page Setup**. The Page Setup dialog box appears. The panels in this dialog box deal mostly with how your document is printed; settings made here don't really affect the worksheet you see on your screen.

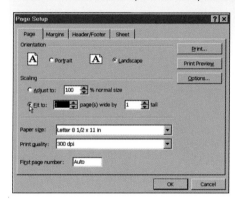

2 Click the Margins Tab

The Margins tab lets you set the four margins on a page, plus margins for a header and footer. Settings are also available to center the page horizontally (left to right) or vertically (up and down). Alter the settings to adjust your document's margins; for example, set the Top, Left, Right, and Bottom margins to **1** to give your document a one-inch margin all the way around. (Click the **Print Preview** button if you want to view the results of your changes.)

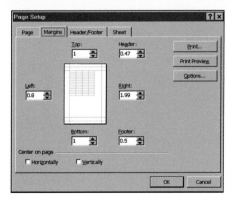

3 Click OK

The margins are set. You'll see them when the document is printed (although the page boundary line shows where page breaks will appear in the printed document).

INSPECTING CAROL DEMOGRAPHICS								
Season Tkts	Adults	Students	Sr.Citizens	Children	Comps	Walk-Ins	**Total**	
30	17	5	13	3	14	17	99	
14	18	1	2	3	1	21	60	
0	0	0	0	0	0	0	0	
7	21	37	5	1	2	5	78	
24	14	7	11	0	5	6	67	
14	134	11	8	6	5	6	184	
21	25	1	8	7	9	5	76	
4	16	5	6	1	9	8	49	
12	22	1	6	1	13	12	67	
14	41	11	12	4	20	22	124	
140	308	79	71	26	78	102	804	

4 Manually Drag Margins

If you'd rather set your margins by eye, open the **File** menu and choose **Print Preview**. The Print Preview page appears.

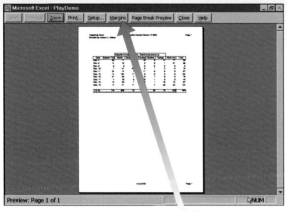

Click

5 Click the Margins Button

Click the **Margins** button; the document preview grows a set of handles that can change margins and column widths; use the mouse to drag any handle. Click the **Margins** button again to return to regular Preview mode; click the **Close** button to close the Print Preview screen. The new margins take effect immediately.

These set column width

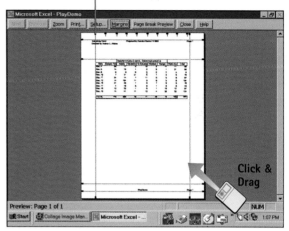

Click & Drag

End

How-To Hints

Printer Margin Limits

Each printer has its own limits on margins. For example, most laser printers cannot print to the outside half-inch of a page; setting a margin to 0 may result in information not being printed. Likewise, ink printers may have a one-quarter–inch top margin but a fat three-quarter–inch bottom margin. You cannot print outside the margin on those printers.

Set Margins for Everything

Margins in Excel are set only for the current worksheet or chart, not for the entire workbook. To set margins for everything, visit every sheet and every chart in the workbook.

Click and Drag Not Accurate

Using **Print Preview** to set margins is nifty in a visual sense, but it's also inaccurate. Use the Page Setup dialog box if you need precise margins.

Let's Visit the Page Setup

Just about anything in Excel that deals with preparing the final document gives you access to the Page Setup dialog box. For example, clicking the **Setup** button in the Print Preview window displays that dialog box.

How to Use Print Preview

You should have heard the giggles when people, long tired of using a typewriter, got their hands on a word processor. Erasing text meant no more white-out or eraser stubble or blanking cartridges. And you could cut and paste! Wow.

Of course, there was a problem when it came to printing. Oftentimes, you needed to print over and over to get the final product looking right; because the screen didn't show you exactly what the final result was, printing wasted lots of paper. The solution? The Print Preview command. Always use **Print Preview** before you print.

1 Choose File, Print Preview

You should use Print Preview to confirm that your document looks the way you want it to look before you print. From the Print Preview screen you can adjust your margins, zoom in on sections of the document, print, or view where the page breaks. Clicking the **Close** button takes you from the Print Preview window into your document for touch ups or formatting.

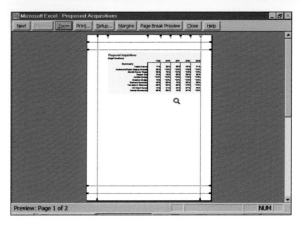

2 Choose View, Page Break Preview

The Page Break Preview command allows you to see where the page break is going to land—the dashed blue border shows you where. If it's not where you want, it can be adjusted.

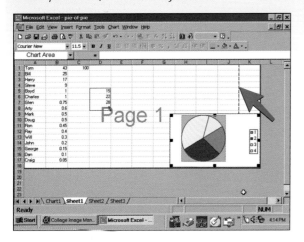

3 Arrange the Breaks

Hover your mouse pointer over the dashed blue border that represents the page break you want to move; your cursor changes to a double-headed arrow, indicating that you can move the border in or out. Click and drag the border as needed.

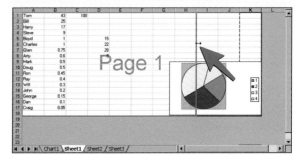

4 Arrange the Page

Drag to move the chart all onto a page (or use the mouse to resize the chart).

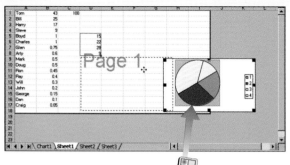

Click & Drag

5 Choose View, Normal

Your document stays in the Page Break Preview screen until you tell Excel to return to Normal view. You can enter, edit, and format in Page Break Preview mode if you like; most people don't because it's easier to see the details of your worksheet in Normal view.

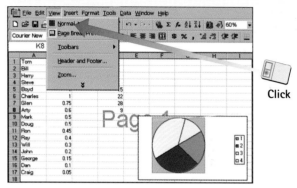

Click

End

How-To Hints

Print Preview Button

You can click the **Print Preview** button on the toolbar for a quick look at your work.

Where's the Rest of It?

Print Preview shows you only the current worksheet, not any charts or other worksheets in the workbook. To preview, click the **Print** button, choose **Entire Workbook** from the Print dialog box, and then click the **Preview** button.

Previewing a Range of Pages

To preview a specific range of pages, click the **Print** button in the Print Preview screen, and then click **Pages**. Type the page numbers you want to preview in the From and To boxes and then click **Preview**.

Dotted Line Indicates Page Break

The dotted line around cells in your document isn't a line of ants off to a picnic. It's placed by the Print or Print Preview command to show you where the next page falls. This can be used as a guideline to adjust your work and stay within one page.

How to Change Printing Orientation

Marcia finally solved her printer's page orientation problem. She put her HP 4000 on a lazy Susan. "Now when I want to print wide," she says, "I simple reorient the printer left to right." She swings the hefty printer around and paper, by golly, sure does come out left to right. But it's not the same thing as true page orientation.

Some information looks best up and down, while other information looks good left to right. In the old days, special printers were made just so that spreadsheets could print long. Today, there are page orientation settings in the Print dialog box. Oh, what an age we live in!

Begin

1 Open the Print Dialog Box

Open the **File** menu and choose **Print**. (The same printer command is used whether you're printing long or short.)

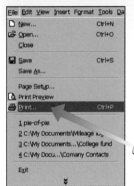

Click

2 Click the Properties Button

Changing the page orientation is the printer's job, not Excel's. Click the **Properties** button in the Print dialog box to display a dialog box for your printer's settings. (Each printer is different, so what you see on your screen may appear subtly different from the images shown in this book.)

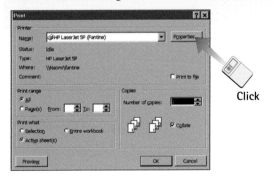
Click

3 Choose Landscape

In the **Paper** tab, click the **Landscape** radio button to print long. Note that no special paper is required; your printer merely prints differently on regular paper. Click **OK** to close your printer's Properties dialog box.

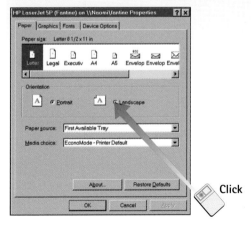
Click

4 Click Preview

Before you print, ensure that Excel got the message by clicking the **Preview** button in the Print dialog box. This displays the Print Preview window, where you can confirm that your document is now long. Click the **Print** button in the Print Preview window; the document spews out of the printer.

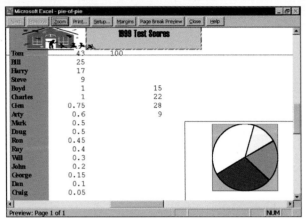

End

How to Print Part of the Worksheet

When they print out that 200-page worksheet at General Motors, do you think they plop the whole thing down on the boss's desk? No, they use a stapler and a pair of scissors to plop down only the most significant parts. Even then, they're being silly because Excel can be told exactly what to print and what not to print. For example, you can print a selected page, the current page, or the entire workbook (instead of only the worksheet).

Begin

1 Print Selected Pages

To print only a few pages in a long worksheet, click the **File** menu and choose the **Print** command to display the Print dialog box. In the Page Range area's From box, enter the first page of the range you want to print; type the last page in the To box. To print a single page, list it in both the From and To boxes. Click **OK**; only the specified pages print.

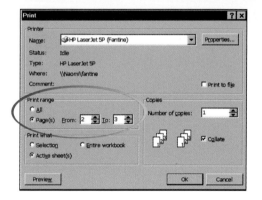

2 Print a Selected Area

Some spreadsheets contain mountains of numbers, but only a small part of that information is useful—a summary or tally. To print only that part of the worksheet, select only those cells you want printed.

Date	Starting	Ending	Total
1-Jan		12575.2	
5-Jan	12575.2	12597.2	22.0
26-Jan	12634.2	12659.2	25.0
Total for January			**47.0**
4-Feb	12701.0	12723.0	22.0
9-Feb	12776.0	12799.1	23.1
17-Feb	12852.1	12874.9	22.8
28-Feb	12927.9	12947.8	19.9
23-Feb	13000.8	13024.3	23.5
Total for February			**111.3**
2-Mar	13057.8	13082.7	24.9
5-Mar	13129.9	13153.5	23.6

1999 Mileage Log

3 Set the Print Area

Open the **File** menu, choose **Print Area**, and select **Set Print Area**. A gray line of ants surrounds the selected cells, indicating that this portion of your worksheet has become the print area. Preview the print area before you print (open the **File** menu and choose **Print Preview**); note that only the print area appears. Click the **Print** button in the Print Preview window to print.

1999 Mileage Log

Date	Starting	Ending	Total	Trip
1-Jan		12575.2		
5-Jan	12575.2	12597.2	22.0	Bank
26-Jan	12634.2	12659.2	25.0	Bank/FedX
Total for January			**47.0**	
4-Feb	12701.0	12723.0	22.0	FedX
9-Feb	12776.0	12799.1	23.1	Bank
17-Feb	12852.1	12874.9	22.8	Bank
28-Feb	12927.9	12947.8	19.9	PO
23-Feb	13000.8	13024.3	23.5	Bank
Total for February			**111.3**	
2-Mar	13057.8	13082.7	24.9	Bank/FedX
5-Mar	13129.9	13153.5	23.6	FedX
11-Mar	13200.7	13224.5	23.8	FedX

4 Print on Only One Page

To get an entire worksheet to print on a single page, open the **File** menu and choose **Page Setup**. In the Page Setup dialog box, click the **Fit to** button and type **1** in the corresponding text box.

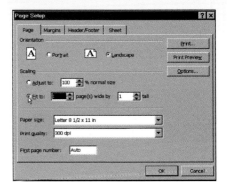

5 View the Results

When you print, Excel squeezes the entire worksheet onto a single page, which makes the print tiny—but that's what you wanted.

6 Print the Entire Workbook

Excel normally prints only the worksheet or chart you're currently viewing. To direct Excel to print an entire workbook, open the **File** menu, choose **Print**, click the **Entire Workbook** option, and click **OK**.

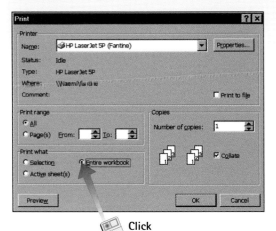

Click

End

How-To Hints

Printing a Selection

There is a difference between selecting and printing cells and creating a print area. When you select cells, it's a one-time thing; you open the **File** menu, choose **Print**, and click the **Selection** radio button. The selected part of the worksheet prints—end of story. If you set a print area, however, it stays set until you clear it. To clear it, open the **File** menu, choose **Print Area**, and select **Clear Print Area**.

Using Page Breaks

If you want printing to stop at a certain point on a page, insert a page break. Select the cell where you want the page to break (Excel breaks the page to the left and top of the cell you select), open the **Insert** menu, and choose **Page Break**. Use the **Print Preview** command to see how the breaks affect your document—that is, which information is printed on which pages. To remove a page break, reselect the cell where you first inserted the break, then open the **Insert** menu and choose **Remove Page Break**. Don't forget that you can edit page breaks in the Page Break Preview mode (refer to Task 5).

How to Print Various Worksheet Elements

The projectionist's name is either "Focus" or "Frame." I'm not certain which, but in most cheesy art-house cinemas, someone shouts "Focus!" whenever the picture looks bad or "Frame!" when you can see the line between the frames (or worse, sprocket holes).

In Excel, the ugly parts of the worksheet don't normally print. Your hard copy doesn't have the cell's gridlines or the row or column headings. But it can! If someone looks at your document and says "Frame," you can give it to him.

Begin

1 Print the Gridlines

In the olden days, worksheets always printed with gridlines. You had to tell Excel to shut them off. Today, the gridlines are off automatically. To turn them on, open the **File** menu, choose **Page Setup**, and click the **Sheet** tab in the Page Setup dialog box. Click the **Gridlines** check box to direct Excel to print gridlines; click **OK**.

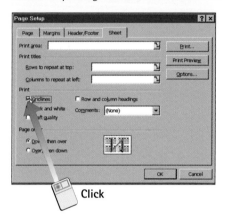

Click

2 View the Results

Either print your document or use the **Print Preview** command to view the results; notice the gridlines.

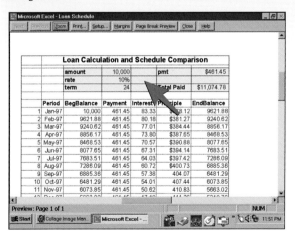

3 Print Headings

The row and column headings in a worksheet can also be printed. This is helpful when you're trying to work out the kinks in a worksheet and need to show someone a hard copy. To configure Excel to print headings, open the **File** menu, choose **Page Setup**, and click the **Sheet** tab in the Page Setup dialog box. Click the **Row and Column Headings** check box to direct Excel to print headings; click **OK**.

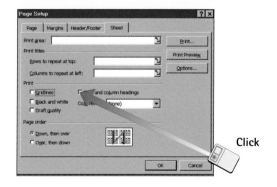

Click

4 View the Results

The row and column headings print when you print the entire document. Use the **Print Preview** command to review the page.

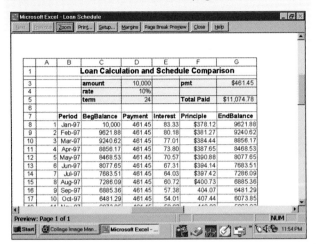

End

Task

9

Excel as a Database

*H*ave you ever wondered why a superhero needs a secret identity? Was it some form of legal protection or a way to avoid paying income tax? Psychologists might say that having a secret identity allows each of us to identify with the superhero. See, with a regular suit, hat, and set of glasses, Superman looked like a common guy. Secret identities might also let us know that we all have certain talents not everyone knows about. For example, that geeky girl in seventh grade seemed kind of hopeless—until she sang in the school chorale. Wow! What talent! Who knew?

Excel has a secret identity. (Actually, Excel has several if you consider its drawing capabilities.) Its most formal secret identity is as a database. Remember, any information that can be stored in rows and columns can fit into a spreadsheet. Building a database in a spreadsheet is another way of applying this row-column logic.

Obviously, if you're going to get into databases, you should probably use a real database program, such as Microsoft Access (which also comes with Office 2000); for information stored in rows and columns—especially information you might be using for regular spreadsheet calculations or a look-up table—Excel is more than suited to the task.

This chapter covers Excel as a database. There are a few tricks you can pull putting information into rows and columns in Excel, plus some special commands for accessing the information stored in the secret-identity database. While it's not really a jack-of-all-trades, Excel can be considered the superhero and its database function, well, a secret identity. ●

How to Create a List of Data (Database)

Excel's database function is described using the term *list*. Not Franz Liszt, or "list" as in "The Titanic is listing to the left," but list as in "a collection of information." It could be as simple as a grocery list, but most often its information is organized into rows and columns—a table. Each column contains a certain type of information: last name, address, pants size, or some other tidbit. The rows contain the records in the database. Excel instantly recognizes a list in a worksheet and offers several interesting functions for dealing with the list—but first, you must create the list.

Begin

1 Start a New Worksheet

Press **Ctrl+N** or click the **New** button on the toolbar to start a new worksheet in Excel. You could also set up a list in an existing worksheet. Make sure the list is separate from other information in the worksheet.

	A	B	C	D	E	F	G	H	I
1	Number	Last name	First name	Party	Terms	DIO?			
2	1	Washington	George	Fed	2	N			

2 Enter Column Labels and Data

The list must start with column labels in the first row. These column labels not only provide a heading for the items in that row, but Excel uses them when you search, sort, or sift through the list. Once you've labeled your columns, type information into each row in the list. The contents of each column should match the column title. When you get to the end of a row, press **Enter** to move to the next one. Any formatting in one row is copied to the next row as you type.

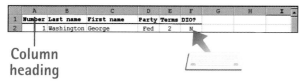

	A	B	C	D	E	F	G	H	I
1	Number	Last name	First name	Party	Terms	DIO?			
2	1	Washington	George	Fed	2	N			

Column heading

3 Save the List

Save the list when you're done entering information. Open the **File** menu, choose **Save As**, and use the Save As dialog box to save the list just as you would any other worksheet in Excel. (See Chapter 1, "Getting Started," for more saving information.)

4 Add a Record

To add a record to the end of the list, press **Ctrl+End** to select the last cell in the list. Click in the first column of the next row and type in the new record. To insert a record into the middle of the table, select the row just below where you want the new record inserted; then open the **Insert** menu and choose **Rows**. Finally, type the information into the row, being careful not to leave any blank cells.

5 Remove a Record

To remove a record from your list, begin by selecting the row that contains the record. Open the **Edit** menu and choose **Delete** to open the Delete dialog box; choose **Shift Cells Up** and click **OK**.

Click

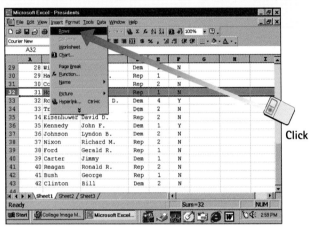

Click

End

How-To Hints

Don't Hide Anything!

Don't use the Hide command to hide a row or column in the middle of a list. If you hide any information in a list, it could be accidentally deleted.

No Blank Rows or Columns

The list should not contain any blank rows or columns, as these mess up how Excel views the list.

No Extra Spaces

Try to avoid typing an extra space before or after items in the list. For example, Excel might not think that "Nixon" matches "Nixon " in your list because of the trailing space. If you're using a space to indent information, consider using the left-indent cell format instead.

Additional Information

If you have any other data or formulas in the worksheet, it's best to put them above or below the list—never to the right or left (which may interfere with the list).

One List Per Worksheet

Excel limits you to one list per worksheet. If you need another list in your workbook, use another worksheet.

How to Sort and Sift the List

The reason information is put into a database is, above all, to have it all in one place. Beyond that, the information can be manipulated by the power of the computer so that you can look at it in different ways.

For example, you can create a list of everyone you know. One column might identify people you work with, another identifies relatives, and a third lists people who owe you money. Using Excel, you can easily sift through that information, trimming the list to just those folks you specify, such as relatives you work with and who owe you money.

Begin

1 Sort the List

Select the column you want to sort by clicking the column heading or selecting a single cell in that column. Then open the **Data** menu and select **Sort** to view the Sort dialog box. You can sort by as many as three criteria; enter the criteria by selecting from the drop-down lists. (Information in these lists is gathered from the table's headings in the worksheet.) Select either **Ascending** (A to Z; smallest to largest) or **Descending** (Z to A; largest to smallest). Click **OK**; the list is sorted to your specifications.

2 Sift Through the List

Sifting lets you see only part of the list based on criteria you select. To sift, create a list in your document, open the **Data** menu, choose **Filter**, and select **AutoFilter**. Each heading in your list sprouts a drop-down list summarizing the entries that appear in that column. Select an entry in a column's drop-down list to display only those records whose entries in that column match the one you selected. (For example, select **Dem** to view a list of Democratic presidents.) To refine your list, choose more columns to sift through, such as Democratic presidents who served more than one term in office.

Click

3 Create a Custom Sifting

When you choose **Custom** from a column's drop-down list, a Custom AutoFilter dialog box appears. You can use it to select specific items from that column. For example, you could choose **Begins With** and then a letter or number.

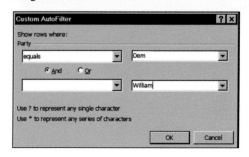

4 Find the Top 10

Choose **Top 10** from a column's drop-down list to open the Top 10 AutoFilter dialog box, where you display the top (or bottom) 10 values in the column. For example, you can find the 10 biggest numbers in a table. (To use this feature, you must choose a column with values, not text.) If you need to view the top 5 (or 3 or 21) values instead of the top 10 values, increase or decrease the value in the spin box in the middle of the dialog box. In addition to being able to view a specific number of items in a list, you can select to view the top *percentage* of items in the list—just use the drop-down list on the right side of the dialog box.

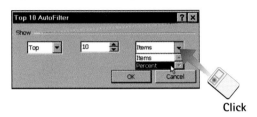

Click

5 Un-Sift

To clear the sifting done by the various AutoFormat headers, choose **All** from the column's drop-down list. Switch off the AutoFilter feature by opening the **Data** menu, choosing **Filter**, and selecting **AutoFilter**. This removes the check mark next to the AutoFilter entry in the menu, returning your list to normal operation.

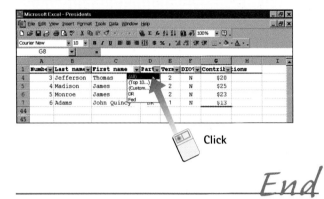

Click

End

How-To Hints

Shortcut Sorting Buttons

There are two toolbar buttons for sorting information: Sort Ascending and Sort Descending. Both buttons have an A, a Z, and an arrow; hover your mouse over each one to determine which is the ascending and which is the descending button. To use them, select a cell in the column you want to sort by and then click the proper button. The rest of the table is sorted along with the column you specify.

Have an Index Column

You notice that the Presidents table contains an index column, showing the president's number, first to most recent. This can come in handy for re-sorting a list such as this to its original order. Without that column, you could sort the list only by the other columns, which may not reorganize it the way it was originally.

How to Search the List

Finding things has its reward, but not everyone is good at it. No one has yet found the Lost Dutchman mine, for example. And look how long it took mankind to find the planet Pluto. Some kids take weeks to find their socks or backpack. Who hasn't lost their keys or glasses?

Fortunately, Excel finds things lickety-split with its Find command—not just in a table, but anywhere in a massive jungle of cells. While your car keys may still be hiding in your pocket and your glasses may be perched atop your head, nothing in your worksheet will ever be lost for long.

Begin

1 Open the Find Dialog Box

Click the **Edit** menu and choose **Find** to open the Find dialog box. This dialog box is your headquarters for locating any lost tidbit of information not just in a list, but in any worksheet. Type the text or value you want to locate in the Find What box and then specify whether Excel should search by rows or columns. Tell Excel what part of the cell it should look in, be it the cell's formula, value, or comments. If the item you're looking for is case sensitive, check **Match Case**. Release the hounds by clicking **Find Next**.

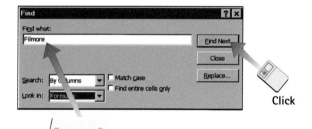

Click

2 Locate the Cell

The cell containing the information you searched for is located and selected. If the information can't be found, Excel tells you so. Click **OK** and try again. (You might need to modify your entry; check its spelling.)

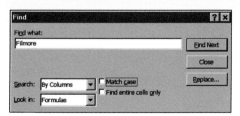

3 Search and Replace

Clicking the **Replace** button in the Find dialog box magically transforms it into the Replace dialog box, which can be used to search for and replace information. Begin by entering the information you want to find in the Find What field; then type the text or value that you want to replace that information in the Replace With field.

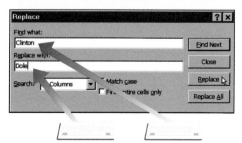

4 Click Find Next

When the text is found, click **Find Next** to find the next occurrence, click **Replace** to replace it, or click **Replace All** to replace every instance of the text. Click the **Close** button to return to your worksheet.

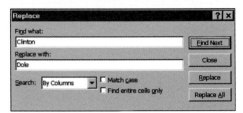

End

How-To Hints

The Find Command Shortcut

The shortcut key for the Find command is **Ctrl+F**. (This shortcut key works for most Windows applications.)

Quick Find Again

If you've closed the Find dialog box, you can quickly find the last thing you searched for by pressing the **F4** key.

How to Use the Data Form

One vision of Hell is as a huge bureaucracy, filled with endless halls and eternal cubicles with countless minions requiring you to fill in forms—in triplicate. There's no carbon paper, but even if there were it wouldn't matter because each form is wickedly different—though it requires the same information.

Excel is not Hell, but it does have forms. When you create a list in a worksheet, Excel also builds a tiny form you can use to scan, search, edit, delete, or enter items into the list. Carbon paper is optional; damnation is not necessary.

Begin

1 Choose Data, Form

Excel examines your worksheet for a list; if there's one found, it displays a data form containing items in the list. (If there's no list found, Excel displays a warning message.) Note that the column headings from the list are displayed along the left side of the dialog box. Use the **Find Prev** and **Find Next** buttons to scan additional records in the list.

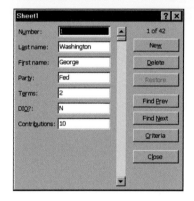

2 Enter a New Record

Click the **New** button to add a new record to the list. The data form goes blank; fill it in. Press **Enter** to add the record.

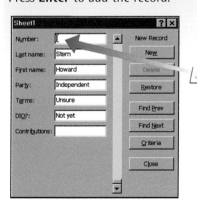

3 Edit a Record

Edit a record by changing the information displayed in the data form's dialog box. Press the **Enter** key after making changes.

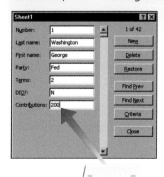

4 Delete a Record

Locate the record you want to delete, highlight the information, and then click the **Delete** button. Excel asks if you're sure—click **OK** to delete or **Cancel** to keep the record.

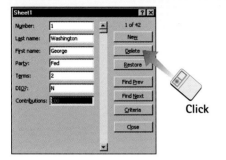

Click

How-To Hints

Sorting After You're Done

After you add a record using the data form, you might want to re-sort the list so that the record fits into the proper place. See Task 2 for information on sorting the list.

5 Search the List

The data form can be used to locate specific records in the list. Begin by clicking the **Criteria** button and then fill in one (or more) of the fields with information you want to match—for example, a city, street, name, or hallucinogen. (Click the **Clear** button to clear out old information or to start over.) Click **Form** to return to the main data form; note that only those records matching the criteria you entered are displayed. (If no matches are found, the Find Prev and Find Next buttons beep when you click them.) Click the **Close** button when you're done using the data form; any changes you've made are reflected on the list.

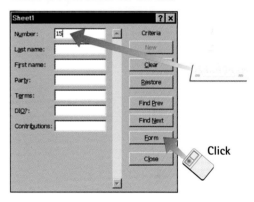

Click

End

Task

10

The Rest of Excel

*T*here are some scientists who try to figure out how things work by blowing them up. It's no joke! After all, sometimes you can't understand how something works unless you take it apart. Some of the things scientists look at are very, very small. To find out what's going on, scientists blow up those teensy doodads (they call them *particles*) and see what pops out.

On the surface this sounds rather crude, but it's understandable. Consider a pocket watch. If we lacked the technology to take it apart, an astute observer could make a guess at how it works by busting it open with a hammer. In the pieces that come out, you could find some gears and maybe a spring, along with other pieces. The gears and spring would be major clues as to the clock's workings. The same thing happens when scientists bust a proton or some other tiny object. Other, even tinier, objects whiz out. It's from those tiny of tiny things that everything is made.

If a scientist were able to explode Excel, a lot of different tiny things would pop out. There would be mathematical formulas, formatting, charts, drawing tools, databases, lists, PivotTables, text and values—a lot of stuff. But wait! There's more...

The final chapter in this book contains a grab bag of stuff, some of it basic and some of it way the heck out there. Some of this stuff you'll use, and other things will wind up in the dustbin, along with the gears and springs that burst forth from all the other computer programs you've blown apart. ●

How to Use More Than One Worksheet

Worksheet. Workbook. Spreadsheet. Welcome to the nomenclature of Excel! *Spreadsheet* refers to the big picture. It's the software. It's Excel. Inside the spreadsheet is a *worksheet*—which is the thing that contains all the rows and columns of cells. The individual worksheets together make a *workbook*. Of course, there can more than one worksheet in a workbook, just like there is more than one page of paper in a textbook. The typical workbook in Excel comes with three worksheets. While you don't need to use them all, each is available. More can be added (or deleted) as needed. This task shows you how to work with multiple worksheets at once.

Begin

1 Switch Between Sheets

To switch from one worksheet to another, use either the **arrow** buttons or the **tabs** at the bottom of the screen. For example, to switch to a different sheet, click that sheet's tab.

Display first sheet   Display next sheet

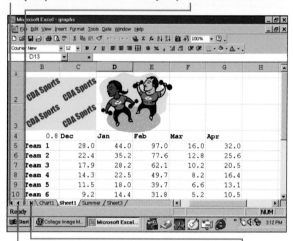

Display preview sheet   Display last sheet

2 Rename a Sheet

Each sheet in your workbook can have its own name, something more clever than Sheet1 or Chart1. That way, it's easier to remember which is which when you're working with multiple sheets. To rename a sheet, click the **tab** of the sheet you want to rename; open the **Format** menu, choose **Sheet**, and select **Rename**. The sheet's name becomes highlighted; type in a new name and press the **Enter** key. Of course, you can also be quick about it by double-clicking the tab, typing the new name, and then pressing **Enter**.

3 Hide a Sheet

To hide a sheet, choose the sheet you want hidden, open the **Format** menu, choose **Sheet**, and then select **Hide**. The worksheet disappears as do its tab from the list. The other worksheets do not renumber themselves—which is a good hint that you have a hidden worksheet in a workbook.

Click

4 Unhide a Worksheet

To unhide a previously hidden worksheet, open the **Format** menu, choose **Sheet**, and select **Unhide**. In the Unhide dialog box, select the sheet you want to unhide from the list and then click **OK**.

5 Add or Remove a Sheet

To insert a new sheet into your workbook, open the **Insert** menu and choose **Worksheet**. The worksheet is inserted after the current worksheet, and is given the name **Sheetx** (where **x** is the number of worksheets now in the workbook). For example, if you currently have five sheets in a workbook and you insert a new sheet, the new sheet is named **Sheet6**. To remove a sheet, right-click its tab, open the **Edit** menu, and choose **Delete Sheet**. Excel asks if you really, *really* want to delete the sheet. Click **OK**.

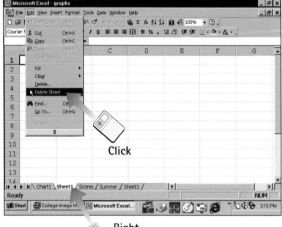

6 Rearrange the Sheets

The worksheets shown on the tabs at the bottom of the window can be in any order you like. To rearrange them, simply drag each tab to a new position. Release the mouse where you want to plop down the sheet.

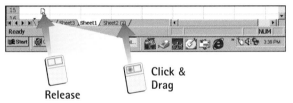

End

Sheet-Switching Shortcuts

You can switch sheets from the keyboard in a workbook by pressing the **Ctrl+Page Up** and **Ctrl+Page Down** keys; **Ctrl+Page Down** displays the next highest number sheet, while **Ctrl+Page Up** displays the next lowest sheet.

Quick Sheet Renaming

Double-click the sheet's **tab** to quickly rename any sheet in the workbook. That selects the name and lets you type a new one.

Zapping Multiple Sheets

You can delete several sheets from a workbook by clicking the worksheets' tabs and then pressing the **Delete** key. **Ctrl+click** to select more than one worksheet tab at a time.

Duplicating Sheets

To create a duplicate of a worksheet in a workbook, press and hold the **Ctrl** key while you drag the sheet's tab. The sheet icon appears with a plus sign on it, letting the world know you're duplicating it. Drag and drop the worksheet to its new position.

How to Reference Data in Other Worksheets

Excel grew separate worksheets in a workbook because somewhere along the line Excel actually had *competition*. (Gasp!) There were *other* spreadsheets you could buy. (Scandalous!) One of them touted itself as the "3D spreadsheet" (huh?), which merely meant that in addition to rows and columns, it had "pages," or separate worksheets. Excel had to have that, too.

There is no rule saying how you should deal with worksheets in a workbook; you can put all your stuff into a single worksheet or into several. If you ever need to reference cells in another worksheet, you need to know one four-letter word: *link*.

Begin

1 Copy the Cell You Want to Link

Select a worksheet that contains a cell you want linked with another cell in another worksheet. This works like copying, except that the information in the copy is updated when the original changes (which is why it's called a *link* and not a *copy*). Click the **Copy** button in the toolbar.

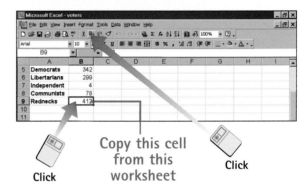

Copy this cell from this worksheet

Click

Click

2 Paste Link the Cell

In the second worksheet, select the cell into which you'll paste the link; open the **Edit** menu, choose **Paste**, and select **Special**. In the Paste Special dialog box, click the **Paste Link** button. That way, you actually are referencing the information in the original cell instead of copying the cell's contents.

Click

3 The Information Is Linked

A link is pasted into the cell you selected in the second worksheet; note that the cell actually references the original worksheet and location.

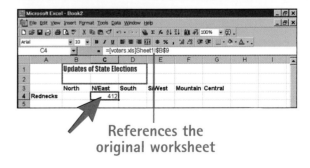

References the original worksheet

4 Manually Enter a Link

You can also manually reference a link to another worksheet. To do so, simply type into the cell the other worksheet's name, followed by an exclamation point and the cell reference. For example, type **Sheet1!A1** to reference cell A1 in Sheet 1. If the cell has a name, you can use its name instead: **Sheet1:Bobs_Salary**.

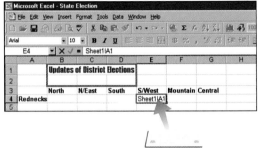

End

How-To Hints

Links Are Updated!

When you link to data in another worksheet, that information is updated in the second worksheet when it's changed in the first—even if it's a worksheet in another file on disk. If you're referencing a list of scores or prices, that information is updated whenever the original cell is updated.

Remember Absolute Addresses

Don't forget to use absolute addresses when you manually enter a link. For example, Sheet1!A1 references cell A1 in Sheet 1, but if you drag-fill that cell, you'll reference other cells in Sheet 1 in addition to A1. To keep the reference to A1 the same, use **Sheet1!$A$1** instead.

Linking Between Workbooks

You can also link between worksheets in separate workbooks. In this case, the reference that is pasted in also includes the original workbook's name on disk, which Excel looks up to see if the data changes—for example, State Election!Sheet1!C3.

How to Insert Foreign Objects

Even though you may never pick up the phone and call, don't you find those 30-minute infomercials interesting? Don't you get engrossed and hyped about a product that is so revolutionary that, well, you're either an idiot for not thinking of it yourself or an idiot for not dialing the 800 number right now?

Try as it might, Excel is not the be-all, end-all product Microsoft thinks it is. If it were, would it not have its own infomercial? Excel can't do everything; for those things you have other software. To bring that point home, you have Excel's Insert Object command.

Begin

1 Open the Object Dialog Box

Select the cell(s) into which you want to insert your object; and open the **Insert** menu and choose **Object**. The Object dialog box contains a smorgasbord of objects that you can paste or create directly in your worksheet. The **Create New** tab shows you various objects that you can create using other software on your PC to be inserted into Excel. Choose **Bitmap Image** from the Object type list to create an image using your Paint program to be inserted into Excel, and then click **OK**.

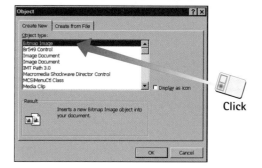

Click

2 Paint Opens

The screen changes: You're still in Excel, but the Paint program's menus, toolbar, and color palette appear. The window floating over the worksheet is where the bitmap image will be created. You can use the handles around the window to resize the object or move the object by dragging its edge.

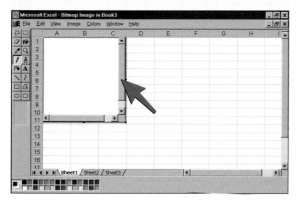

3 Create an Image

Use the tools in Paint to make an image in the Object window.

Click

4 Return to Excel

When you are finished and want to return to Excel, simply click outside of the Paint image (somewhere in the worksheet). Paint vanishes and you're returned to Excel. The image remains as an object in the worksheet.

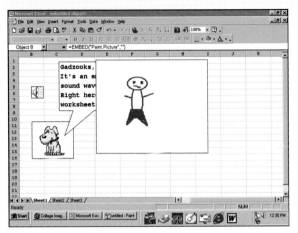

5 Edit the Object

You can edit an object by double-clicking it; that reruns the program that created the object, allowing you to touch things up. Click in the worksheet to return to Excel.

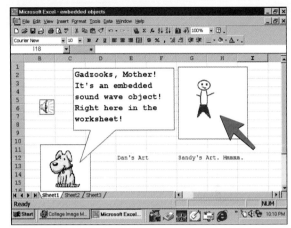

End

How-To Hints

Different Types of Objects

Different programs in the Objects dialog box create different types of objects. For example, if you select to create a WAV sound object, a program for recording sound appears. When you use it to record a sound, it then inserts the sound as an object in the document; double-click the **object** in the sheet to play the sound.

Embedding as an Icon

If you choose the **Display as Icon** item in the Objects dialog box, the final result of your effort is displayed as an icon—not an image—in the worksheet. To edit, view, or play the object, double-click the **icon**.

If You Right-Click...

Right-clicking an embedded option displays a pop-up menu that lets you do various interesting things, including edit or view the object.

Removing an Object

To delete an **object**, click it once to select it and press the **Delete** key. Poof! It's gone.

How to Create and Use a Macro

Macros are a scary and advanced subject, but they're also something many Excel users rave about. In a nutshell (which is where most advanced subjects should be kept), a *macro* is a program you can write or record in Excel. Running the macro carries out the instructions you wrote or recorded, automating some task or drudgery.

Macros are not for the foolhardy. In fact, macros in Excel are written in a programming language called Visual Basic for Applications (VBA), which many folks devote a great chunk of their lives to learning. You don't have to! But if you're curious, this task should whet your appetite.

Begin

1 Open the Record Macro Dialog Box

To record a macro, open the **Tools** menu, choose **Macro**, and select **Record New Macro**. The Record Macro dialog box appears. Use it to set a shortcut key for your macro (optional), to specify where the macro should be stored, to enter a description, and to name the macro. The macro's name must start with a letter; it can contain numbers and symbols but not spaces. (Excel lets you know if you goof the name.) Above all, it should be named something useful; a good rule of thumb is to think of macros as *verbs* (the name should represent something that you're doing). When you finish with this dialog box, click **OK**.

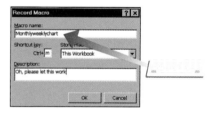

2 Begin Recording

Excel transforms into macro-recording mode, where it pays attention to every detail of everything you do. Obviously, doing something you want to repeat is the goal here. (Note: To stop recording, click the **Stop** button. To use relative references as opposed to absolute references, click the button on the right. For more information about absolute and relative references, see Chapter 2, Task 6, "How to Fill Groups of Cells.")

3 Carry Out a Task

The task you record should be something you expect to repeat often. Enter some information in a column for this example. To start, select cell **A2** and type **Week 1**. Drag-fill down five rows to name cells Week 2 through Week 5. Click cell **B1** and type **Sunday**, drag-fill across six rows to name cells Monday through Saturday, and finally, click to select cell **B2**. Click **Stop** when you're finished with the task you want to record. The macro stops recording and is saved in the location you specified in the Record Macro dialog box.

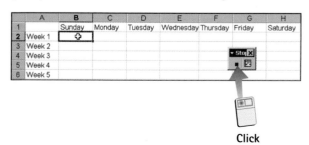

Click

4 Run a Macro

Open the **Tools** menu, choose **Macro**, and click **Macros**. The Macro dialog box is displayed. In it, you can see macros you've created; you can run or delete macros. (You can even edit if you know VBA.)Select a macro from the list (such as the one you created earlier in this task) and click **Run**.

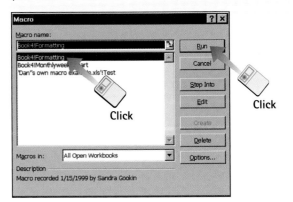

Click

5 The Macro Runs

The macro runs, carrying out the instructions you recorded. In this example, cells A2–A6 are named Week 1–Week 5, cells B1–H1 are named Sunday–Saturday, and cell B2 is selected.

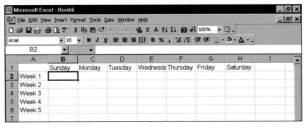

Click

End

How-To Hints

The Macro Keyboard Shortcut

Press **Alt+F8** to quickly summon the Macro dialog box. This is entirely un-memorable, but you'll get used to it if you mess with macros a lot. Alternatively, (as mentioned earlier) you can assign a keyboard shortcut.

Macro Boo-Boos

If you record a macro and find upon playback that it either doesn't work the way you like or that it produces an error, just delete it. If the Visual Basic editing window appears, close it; then, in the Macro dialog box, select your macro and delete it. Re-record it to create a new one

How to Create an HTML Document in Excel

HTML, Hypertext Mark-up Language, consists of codes used to format Web pages on the Internet. HTML comes in handy for sharing information in certain circumstances, such as over a network. While you could create an entire Web page using Excel, there are tools on the market better for that. Excel is a full-time spreadsheet; it only moonlights as an HTML editor. No matter what type of editor you use, however, formatting does become important with HTML pages.

Begin

1 Create a Worksheet

The task in creating an HTML document is the same as creating any old worksheet: Do it!

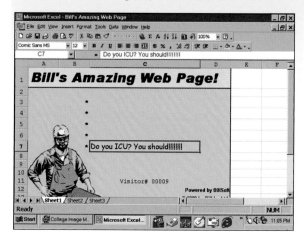

2 Insert a Hyperlink

Web pages (and now, Excel worksheets) mark themselves by way of their links. You can insert a link into a worksheet even if you don't plan on saving it as a Web page. To do so, select the **cell** that will contain the link (the cell need not contain text) and then open the **Insert** menu and choose **Hyperlink**. If the cell is formatted, inserting the link will change the formatting (which you can then redo later).

Click

3 Enter a File Link

Enter the text that you want the viewer to click in order to link to a new page in the Insert Hyperlink dialog box's Text to Display field. Optionally, click the **ScreenTip** button to enter text that will appear when the viewer hovers his mouse pointer over the link. If you know the path to the file to which you want link, enter it in the Type the File or Web Page Name field. If you've recently opened the file or inserted a link to it, click it in the **Or Select from List** pane. (Click **Recent Files**, **Browsed Pages**, or **Inserted Links** to display different files or Web sites.) Alternatively, click the **File** button.

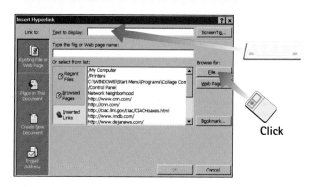

Click

4 Select a File

Use the Link to File dialog box the same way you would use an Open dialog box: Locate and select a file to link to and click **OK** when you've found it.

Choose All Files from this list to display all types of files

Click

5 Click the Link

The link appears in Excel as blue text. Click the blue text to view the linked file. If the link is to another file, that file is loaded. If the link is to a Web page, Windows starts your Web browser, connects to the Internet, and displays the page. (See the How-To Hints for more information about linking to Web pages.)

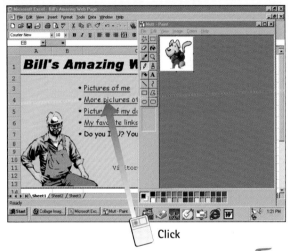

Click

End

How-To Hints

Reformatting Cells

After inserting a hyperlink into a cell, the cell's function changes: Clicking the cell activates the link. In order to do anything to the cell (such as reformat it), you should right-click it and choose the proper command from the menu that pops up.

Entering a Web Page Link

To link to a page on the Web, click the **Web Page** button in the Insert Hyperlink dialog box (refer to step 3). This starts your computer's Web browser; use it to find the page on the Internet to which you will link. When you find the page, return to Excel and click the **OK** button in the Insert Hyperlink dialog box. Don't forget to close the browser window and log off the Internet when you're done.

Removing a Link

To remove a link, right-click the cell containing the link. Choose **Hyperlink**, **Remove Hyperlink** from the pop-up menu that appears.

Saving the Web page

To save an Excel document as a Web page, open the **File** menu and choose **Save as Web Page**. This saves the worksheet twice—once as a regular Excel document and again as a Web page (HTML) document.

Glossary

absolute reference A specific cell whose address does not change if you copy-fill or drag a formula. The absolute reference always uses a specific cell or group of cells.

active cell The cell that has been selected for use or that is currently being used. Excel automatically highlights the active cell.

active worksheet The worksheet that is currently being used.

ascending To go from first to last, smallest to biggest, or A to Z.

AutoCalculate An Excel feature that allows you to drag over a range of numbers to display the total of these numbers.

AutoFill A feature that allows you to create a series of incremental values by dragging the fill handle with the mouse, such as days of the week or numbers.

bar graph A type of chart that compares values in a series, such as months or days.

cell A holding place for information. Cells can contain values, text, formulas, and even graphical images.

cell address The location of a cell on a worksheet, given by column letter and row number.

chart sheet A worksheet that holds only a chart.

Chart Wizard A helper program that walks you through the steps of developing a chart.

clear To remove the cell information, the cell's formatting, or both.

Clipboard A temporary holding area for things that are cut or copied.

close To remove a document or worksheet from the screen.

Collect and Paste A feature that allows you to copy (or cut) up to 12 bits of copied or cut information of a worksheet, collecting them in a special Clipboard. The chunks can be pasted together or one at a time.

column A vertical stack of cells in a spreadsheet.

column heading Located across the top of a worksheet. The columns are lettered from A through Z, AA through ZZ, and so on.

copy To make an exact duplicate of an item, which may be numbers, text, or an image.

crunch The sound a computer makes when it works with numbers.

cursor The point on the screen where you will insert text. The cursor is usually a flashing vertical bar.

cut To remove the selected information.

data region Any bit of filled cell space grouped into a four-sided region.

database An organized collection of information, such as a list of names and addresses.

decrement   The amount by which a number (or variable) is decreased.

delete   To remove the information from a cell

descending   To go from last to first, biggest to smallest, or Z to A.

disk   A magnetic storage device used to store or save information on the computer.

drag   To move an object on the screen by pulling it with the mouse.

Equal button   Located by the Formula bar, this button activates Formula Input mode.

Excel   Spreadsheet program designed by Microsoft. Designed after its predecessors, VisiCalc and Lotus 1-2-3.

exploding pie chart   A type of pie chart that allows you to separate (literally drag) a piece of the information from the chart.

filename   The name given to a file that represents the information in the file.

fill handle   The small plus sign at the lower-right corner of a cell.

floating palette   A tiny window of commands or buttons. The palette can be dragged anywhere on screen.

Formatting toolbar   The toolbar that contains icons used to arrange text and numberic information.

formula   A sequence of values, cell references, names, functions, or mathematical operators that produces a new value.

Formula bar   The box next to the equal sign that displays the formula in the active cell. It can also be used to enter or edit values and formulas.

gridlines   Lines that separate columns and rows.

handles   Small black squares located around the edges of a graphic image, used to resize an object.

hard return   The Alt+Enter combination used to enter more than one line in a cell.

hodge-podge   A variety of stuff.

horizontal scrollbar   The scrollbar located at the bottom of the worksheet. It is used to move the image in the window left or right.

IF   The IF formula compares values and displays other values or formulas as a result.

marching ants   What appears to be around a cell when you select the cell to be copied or cut.

maximize   To increase the size of a window. A maximized window fills the entire screen, or is as large as it can be.

menu bar   The area at the top of the screen the contains menus, all of which have submenus or commands.

minimize   To shrink or reduce a window to the size of an icon on the taskbar or Windows desktop.

Name box   Displays the address of the selected cell.

Num Lock   The key on the keyboard that activates the numeric keypad.

Office Assistant   The helper in Excel that answers your questions and gives gentle, unprompted advice to help you with your current operation.

paste   The process of placing the information that was copied or cut in its new spot.

percentage   Mathematical equations that show how many items per 100 there are. For example, 50 out of 100 is 50 percent.

pie chart   A type of spreadsheet graph that is best used when displaying information that is a portion of a whole.

PivotTable   A table that analyzes information from a variety of lists and tables.

range   A term used to describe a series of things, such as numbers. It also refers to a block of cells in a spreadsheet.

reference   The location of a cell in a worksheet.

relative reference   A cell address in a spreadsheet that relates to the addresses of other cells, rows, or columns.

right-click To click the right mouse button rather than the left.

rows Located down the left side of a worksheet, rows are horizontal cells stacked side by side. They are numbered from 1 to almost infinity.

scientific notation A scientific (or E) notation expresses large values that are too long to fit into a cell.

scrap An item on the Clipboard, cut or copied from a worksheet.

sheet tabs The tabs at the bottom of the worksheet, representing the different sheets in your workbook.

sheets Slang for worksheets, which make up a workbook. *See also* worksheet.

sort To organize according to some pattern or rule. Sorting can be alphabetical or numeric, ascending or descending.

split bar The vertical or horizontal bar that can be dragged to split the screen either vertically or horizontally.

Start button The button that brings up the Start menu.

styles A collection of formatting and character attributes that are put together in one document.

SUM Excel feature that calculates the result of adding all the cells in a row, column, or group.

table A way of organizing data or text in rows and columns.

template A master document for Excel that is used as the starting point or rough draft for other workbooks.

toolbar Contains commands that are represented as icons. Click the icon to begin the command.

value Number information that is used in Excel.

vertical scrollbar The scrollbar on the right side of the screen. Manipulating the scrollbar with your mouse allows you to move information up or down in a window.

Windows Short for Microsoft Windows. Windows is your computer's operating system. It's the program that enables Excel to work.

workbook A collection of worksheets, which can be saved to disk (or opened from disk if it is previously saved).

worksheet The series of cells and grids that you work with.

World Wide Web (WWW) A program that organizes related information together on the Internet.

Index

Get FREE books and more...when you register this book online for our Personal Bookshelf Program

http://register.samspublishing.com/

SAMS

Register online and you can sign up for our *FREE Personal Bookshelf Program...*unlimited access to the electronic version of more than 200 complete computer books—immediately! That means you'll have 100,000 pages of valuable information onscreen, at your fingertips!

Plus, you can access product support, including complimentary downloads, technical support files, book-focused links, companion Web sites, author sites, and more!

And you'll be automatically registered to receive a *FREE subscription to our weekly email newsletter* to help you stay current with news, announcements, sample book chapters, and special events including, sweepstakes, contests, and various product giveaways!

We value your comments! Best of all, the entire registration process takes only a few minutes to complete, so go online and get the greatest value going—absolutely FREE!

Don't Miss Out On This Great Opportunity!